TOBACCO U.S.A.

THE INDUSTRY BEHIND THE SMOKE CURTAIN

EILEEN HEYES

Twenty-First Century Books
Brookfield, Connecticut

To Rob, Jeremy, and Christo

Library of Congress Cataloging-in-Publication Data
Heyes, Eileen.
Tobacco USA : the industry behind the smoke curtain / by Eileen Heyes.
p.   cm.
Includes bibliographical references and index.
Summary: Describes how the health dangers of tobacco became known, despite the political clout and promotional rhetoric that once kept the tobacco industry thriving.
ISBN 0-7613-0974-8 (lib. bdg.)
1. Tobacco–United States–History–Juvenile literature. 2. Tobacco–Health aspects–United States–Juvenile literature. 3. Social change–United States–Juvenile literature. 4. Antismoking movement–United States–Juvenile literature. [1. Tobacco industry–History. 2. Tobacco. 3. Social change. 4. Antismoking movement.] I. Title.
HD9135.H44   1999
338.2'7371'0973–dc21   99-19533   CIP

Cover photograph courtesy of Bernstein & Andriulli © Peter Stallard
Photographs courtesy of Dwane Powell, Raleigh News & Observer.
Distributed by Los Angeles Times Syndicate. Reprinted by permission: pp. 11 (© 1997), 86 (© 1998), 113 (© 1988), 130 (© 1993); SuperStock: pp. 15, 67; The Granger Collection: pp. 21, 22, 33, 37, 42; Corbis/Bettmann: pp. 28, 34; UPI/Corbis-Bettmann: pp. 44, 80; Rothco Cartoons: pp. 50 (Wicks, The Signal, CA), 56 (Kirk, The Toledo Blade, OH), 96 (© Liederman); Archive Photos: pp. 53 (Arnold Sachs/CNP), 88 (Reuters/Robb Wright); PhotoEdit: pp. 92 (© Michael Newman), 103 (© Bonnie Kamin)

Editor: Jean E. Reynolds
Book Design: Victoria W. Monks
Photo Research: Anne Burns

Published by Twenty-First Century Books
A Division of The Millbrook Press, Inc.
2 Old New Milford Road
Brookfield, Connecticut 06804
Visit us at our Web site–http://www.millbrookpress.com

Contents

Acknowledgments

Many people helped me gather and interpret the information in this book, giving generously of their time and attention.

Jackie Thompson and his mother, Louise A. Thompson, welcomed me into their home, shared stories of life in tobacco country, and showed me how flue-cured tobacco is raised, cured, and auctioned. Ray Stanley and Everett Suitt taught me how a crop is started.

Albert G. "Toby" Lee showed me what goes on in the auction warehouse. Arnold Hamm and Mike Lynch of the Flue-Cured Tobacco Cooperative Stabilization Corporation educated me on what happens to tobacco after it leaves auction, and Charlie Finch of the Stabilization Corporation helped me get in touch with other people in the industry. Blake Brown of North Carolina State University explained tobacco economics to me.

Reporters Bob Williams and Catherine Clabby of *The News & Observer* (Raleigh, N.C.) helped me find sources of information and put what I learned in perspective, and Bob ferreted out some factual errors in my manuscript. Julia Carol of Americans for Nonsmokers' Rights, Sally Malek of Project ASSIST, Sarah Elsner of the Survivors and Victims of Tobacco

Empowerment project, Melissa Albuquerque of the Centers for Disease Control and Prevention, and Anthony Pedicini of the Florida Pilot Program on Tobacco Control provided information on the anti-smoking movement and directed me toward other sources. Edward Sweda of the Tobacco Control Resource Center and Tobacco Products Liability Project cleared up some facts about the legal fights.

Dale Coats, John Tackett, and the staff of the Duke Homestead and Tobacco Museum shared insights and gave me access to that facility's collection of early cigarette ads.

Jean Okumura Yamaguchi informed me about smoking trends in Japan.

Maria Thoenen did more than her share of carpool driving so I could spend long afternoons at my computer keyboard. And my wonderful husband and sons patiently listened to me talk about tobacco for most of a year.

To all of these people, I am deeply grateful.

Eileen Heyes

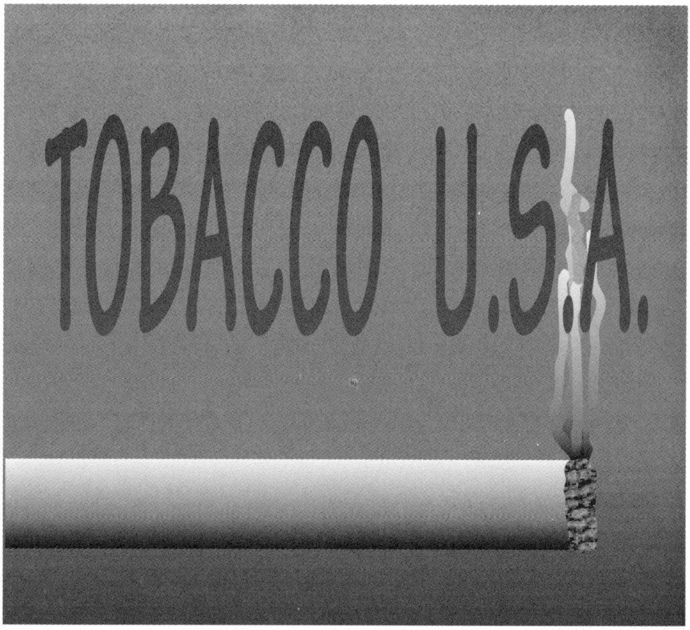
TOBACCO U.S.A.

Chapter One

THE TRAITOR

 On a sweltering summer day in Miami, Florida, the top executive of a cigarette company turned up the heat on his counterparts at other firms.

Bennett LeBow, owner of the Liggett Group, stepped to the witness stand in Dade County circuit court on July 21, 1997. He swore to speak truthfully and then told the jury something no American tobacco company executive had ever publicly admitted under oath: "We believe, for many people, smoking is very addictive."

Does smoking, he was asked, cause lung cancer, heart and lung diseases, and emphysema?

"The answer is yes."[1]

LeBow's testimony was not a surprise: He had been negotiating with lawyers over this admission for more than a year. But his blunt statement in open court symbolized the dramatic turnaround the previous three years had brought in the long-running conflict among cigarette makers, legislators, health advocates, and the public. For four decades, while thousands of scientific studies indicted cigarettes as powerfully addictive and the cause of deadly diseases, tobacco industry executives had hung together in denials. Statistics did not prove anything, industry spokesmen insisted. Tobacco use was a choice, they said, not an addiction. After all, millions of smokers had quit. In the spring of 1994, the top executives of the seven biggest tobacco companies in the United States—including the chief executive officer of Liggett—had stood together before a congressional subcommittee and sworn that they believed these things.

But in 1996, Liggett broke ranks.

Liggett & Myers, as the firm was previously known, had been one of the biggest cigarette makers when its Chesterfield brand commanded a quarter of the American cigarette market in the mid-1920s. But Liggett's position in the industry had slipped, and by the mid-1990s it was the smallest of the five leading U.S. cigarette firms and was struggling to survive; all of its brands combined accounted for less than 2 percent of cigarette sales.

When twenty-two states sued the tobacco industry to recover money spent on medical care for smokers, the Liggett Group defied the industry's long-standing united front and agreed to release thousands of company reports, memos, and other documents. The other firms mounted an intense legal battle to keep the papers secret. But it was a losing fight.

Documents that Liggett released in the spring of 1997 revealed that tobacco executives and company scientists believed in the 1950s that smoking caused

A Dwane Powell cartoon from the Raleigh, North Carolina, newspaper, The News & Observer, *reacts to the admission by Liggett's top executive that smoking is indeed harmful to humans. Previously, the industry had maintained a united front in denying the relationship between smoking and illness— but Liggett's chief is shown revealing the gruesome truth.*

cancer; that the companies had worked out marketing plans designed to appeal to particular ethnic groups; and that they had actively marketed cigarettes to teenagers. And in July, Bennett LeBow himself testified in court that the industry's major cigarette makers, often collectively called Big Tobacco, knew and had known for a long time how cigarettes can harm humans. At the same time, similar papers from the files of other companies were finding their way into the light.

VOICE . . . OF CHANGE

"We at Liggett know and acknowledge that, as the Surgeon General and respected medical researchers have found, cigarette smoking causes health problems, including lung cancer, heart and vascular disease and emphysema. We at Liggett also know and acknowledge that, as the Surgeon General, the Food and Drug Administration and respected medical researchers have found, nicotine is addictive. . . .

"Liggett acknowledges that the tobacco industry markets to 'youth,' which means those under eighteen years of age. . . . Liggett condemns this practice."

Bennett LeBow, owner, Liggett Group Inc., maker of Eve, Lark, and Chesterfield cigarettes, March 20, 1997

What followed over the next year and a half was the remarkable public battering of an industry that was once considered—and that seemed to consider it-self—invulnerable. Lawmakers in Congress who had long been allies of the tobacco industry hesitated or flatly refused to protect it from attacks. Even smokers called for governmental controls over the industry.

Why had Big Tobacco's fortunes changed so much?

For one thing, smoking in the United States had declined sharply: In 1966 almost 43 percent of American adults smoked; by 1997 that figure had fallen to about 25 percent. So not only had the tobacco industry lost much of its support among consumers, but politicians saw that sticking up for Big Tobacco was not going to win them many elections. President Bill Clinton, the first actively antismoking American president, pressed for regulation of tobacco. And in the courts, lawsuits filed by the states proved harder to overcome than the many earlier suits pursued by individuals.

Decades of pent-up and growing hostility toward the industry, it seemed, were coming to a head. Tobacco executives, accustomed to legal, legislative, and economic successes, reacted with surprise. Steven F. Goldstone, chief executive of the company that owned giant R. J. Reynolds Tobacco, conceded in May 1998: "We did underestimate the emotional content—how angry people have been over this issue."[2]

That anger fuels rhetoric that often portrays Big Tobacco in simplistic terms and casts the anti-tobacco movement as a battle of Good versus Evil. But the tobacco industry is complex, touching the lives of Americans in many different ways. To understand what has happened to the tobacco industry and what may lie ahead, it is useful to peer through the smoke at tobacco's long entwinement in the history of our own nation and the industry's current place in the United States and the world.

Chapter Two

Rising Smoke

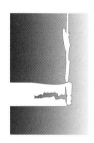

Tobacco wasn't always reviled. Once, it was revered.

The earliest peoples of the continents we now call North and South America considered tobacco sacred. Although there were many different peoples in the Americas, with a wide variety of lifestyles and social customs, virtually all used tobacco. Even nomadic societies that did not practice any other kind of farming grew tobacco. The plant was cultivated as far south as Chile and as far north as the St. Lawrence River.

Early Native Americans made tobacco part of their cultural life in ways that may be difficult to understand today. They considered the mind-altering effects of some plants to be a form of communication with the world of the spirits. They believed that hallucinogenic plants had supernatural powers and that the hallucinations the plants caused meant the user was taking in some of the plant's power and experiencing sacred visions. Researchers think that in early times tobacco contained much more nico-

Tobacco, often used in rituals involving a pipe, was an important part of Native American culture. Historians believe that the Indian name for this type of pipe, tobaca *or* tobago, *may be the origin of the English word "tobacco."*

tine than today's variety, so its use brought much stronger effects.

The main user of tobacco in native cultures was the shaman, who was a spiritual leader and healer. Because illness was thought to have supernatural causes, healing and religion were closely linked. The shaman would blow tobacco smoke over the body of an ill person to diagnose a problem, or blow it onto the skin to drive out the evil that caused the sickness. The leaves were used to ease pain, cure toothaches and earaches, treat snakebites, and clean wounds. In various parts of the Americas, native peoples used tobacco to treat asthma, fevers, indigestion, worms, cysts, coughs, and other ailments.

Religious ceremonies sometimes began with ritual tobacco smoking. Some native peoples believed they could make their land more fertile or acquire other blessings by using tobacco smoke to send messages to the spirits. They smoked tobacco to summon friendly spirits or keep evil spirits away. A Creek tradition holds that tobacco first grew on the spot where a man and a woman fell in love, and because of this genesis in happiness the leaves were smoked as a gesture of peace and friendship. The plant figured in the creation myths of many societies.

When European explorers arrived in what they called the New World, they found the native peoples smoking and chewing tobacco, as well as using it in snuff, drinks, and enemas. In October 1492, Arawak natives offered Columbus a bunch of dried tobacco leaves as a gift. The Europeans had never seen the plant and could not begin to understand its meaning to the people who offered it to them.

Nonetheless, the newcomers were impressed with the ways these strange leaves were used in healing, and they eagerly took news of tobacco home. The most respected physician in Seville, Spain, gave tobacco fine publicity in 1571 by putting out a history of New World plants in which he called tobacco "this holy herb" and wrote that it could cure ailments ranging from toothache to cancer.[1] Jean Nicot, France's ambassador to Portugal in the late 1500s, promoted tobacco's use among French royalty. The plant was given the botanical name *Nicotiana* in his honor. In England, tobacco was supported by Thomas Hariot, a respected scientist who went with the first English colonists to the New World. Hariot became addicted to tobacco and died of cancer of the nose. It was the first documented smoking-related cancer death.

From around 1575 to 1630, Europeans introduced tobacco in Asia, the Middle East, and Africa. By the middle of the seventeenth century, tobacco was recognized around the world not only as a useful substance but also as a crop that could be sold for profit.

Some critics claimed tobacco use could leave men sterile, and religious leaders in Europe couldn't agree on whether it was a holy herb or the food of the devil. King James I of England, a passionate hater of tobacco, tried to suppress its use by raising import taxes by 4,000 percent. His reaction was mild compared to those of some other seventeenth-century rulers. The czar of all the Russias exiled tobacco users to frosty Siberia. The emperor of Hindustan had smokers' lips split. Those who sold tobacco in China were executed. And in Turkey, the sultan punished tobacco users by having a pipe driven through their noses and beheading them.

But nothing stopped the growth of tobacco's popularity. Along with cane sugar, coffee, and chocolate, it was regarded as a great treasure from the New World. One reason tobacco caught on was that it could suppress hunger. This made it appealing to the rural poor in Europe, who were chronically hungry. Some thought it could prevent the deadly disease called the plague. In the American colonies, nearly everyone smoked—even children as young as seven. Eventually, rulers in various lands figured out that rather than try to stop tobacco, they could tax it and bring substantial amounts of gold into their nations' treasuries.

Early in the seventeenth century, Englishman John Rolfe, a leader in the Jamestown settlement in what is now Virginia, planted a type of tobacco seed he had gotten from a Spanish colony in the New World. The leaf of this strain proved to be less harsh and bitter than what the English had been smoking up to that point. Thus was born the tobacco industry in pre-Revolutionary America. Tobacco took on great economic importance to the colonists. It was sometimes used as money. For 150 pounds (68 kilograms) of tobacco, a colonist could have a woman to marry brought over from England.

Over the course of the eighteenth century, slave labor made it possible for tobacco farms to become

VOICES . . . FROM THE PAST

"And now good Country men, let us (I pray you) consider, what honor or policy can move us to imitate the barbarous and beastly manners of the wild, godless, and slavish Indians, especially in so vile and stinking a custom? . . . Why do we not as well imitate them in walking naked as they do? . . .

"Have you not reason then to be ashamed, and to forbear this filthy novelty, ... A custom loathsome to the eye, hateful to the Nose, harmful to the brain, dangerous to the Lungs, and in the black stinking fume thereof, nearest resembling the horrible Stygian smoke of the pit that is bottomless."

James I, "A Counterblaste to Tobacco," 1604

"Tobacco, divine, rare, superexcellent tobacco, which goes far beyond all the panaceas, potable gold, and philosophers' stones, a sovereign remedy to all diseases...but as it is commonly abused by most men, which take it as tinkers do ale, 'tis a plague, a mischief, a violent purger of goods, lands, health, hellish, devilish and damned tobacco, the ruin and overthrow of body and soul."

Robert Burton, "The Anatomy of Melancholy," 1621

19

plantations. The American colonies became one of the world's biggest tobacco suppliers. British rulers controlled the colonies' tobacco trade with a heavy hand, knowing how much the colonists depended on the income they earned by exporting tobacco. It became a significant source of friction, one of many that led eventually to the Revolutionary War.

In the nineteenth century, a new way of drying tobacco leaves was discovered. The harvested leaves had to be dried, or cured, in heated barns. In 1839 an eighteen-year-old slave in Caswell County, North Carolina, tried fueling the curing barn fire with charcoal instead of the usual wood. As a result of the increased heat, the leaves turned a brilliant gold, lighter in look and taste than the dark leaf produced in coastal Virginia. The golden tobacco from this inland section of North Carolina and neighboring Virginia was called Bright Leaf. About thirty years later, a mutant strain of tobacco with pale-colored leaves appeared in Ohio; the plant was called White Burley. It quickly spread to Kentucky and Tennessee, where farmers cured it with natural air instead of heat. The two would become the dominant American tobaccos.

By the middle of the nineteenth century, tobacco smokers in Europe had begun to roll cured leaf into small smokes that the Spanish called *cigaritos.* Because the ingredients were easy to carry in small pouches, the little cigarettes became a favorite of soldiers who found that they made the tension of the battlefield easier to bear. In England a tobacconist named Philip Morris promoted cigarettes to young adults from

The American tobacco industry relied on slave labor, an economic reality not only accepted but encouraged by the British. In this engraved English tobacco label from around 1730, the company shows a Virginia planter at ease while his slaves labor in the tobacco field.

upper-class families by naming his brands after prestigious universities. By the millennium's end, his name would come to be synonymous with the power of Big Tobacco.

Americans were the world's biggest consumers of tobacco in the mid-nineteenth century, but chewing was still far more popular than smoking. Richmond, Virginia, became the manufacturing center, with fifty tobacco factories run with slave labor. By the time of the Civil War, in the 1860s, tobacco use was so thoroughly taken for granted that Confederate soldiers were given some leaf along with their food rations. Union soldiers fighting in the South tried Bright Leaf and found it to their liking. After the war they sent word to North Carolina that they wanted to buy some.

In the tiny village of Durham's Station, North Carolina, a veteran named Washington Duke returned from the Civil War to find his farm looted, except for a barn full of tobacco. He packed his nine-year-old son, James Buchanan Duke, and the leaf onto a wagon and set out to sell or barter the tobacco for whatever he could get. It took only one selling season for the Dukes to see that their fortune lay not in the backbreaking work of raising the tobacco, but in packaging and selling it. That nine-year-old boy, known as Buck, would grow up to create, almost single-handedly, the huge corporate octopus called the tobacco industry.

Wash Duke built a factory in Durham to package tobacco. Other factories were springing up around the same time in the area. The most successful tobacco business at the time was Bull Durham, whose owners opened an auction market for farmers and built warehouses with the intention of making Durham the capital of the tobacco-growing region known as the Bright Belt. Factory-made cigarettes were rare. Most people rolled their own, and Bull Durham sold cigarette tobacco in little sacks.

A tobacco advertising poster from around 1885, featuring the Dukes, father and son. Young James Buchanan Duke would later become the leading force behind the American Tobacco Company—a trust that eventually gained control of 90 percent of the entire industry.

Duke's business grew and prospered. With it, Buck Duke grew into a shrewd and driven business-man. In 1880, Buck Duke became the head of a firm his father renamed W. Duke Sons & Company. By that same year, two entrepreneurs named Allen & Ginter had caught the public's fancy with ready-made cigarettes they packaged with little trading cards that children could collect.

The year 1880 held another, far more important change for the fledgling cigarette industry. A Virginia youth named James Albert Bonsack got a patent that year for a machine that could roll about two hundred cigarettes a minute—what forty to fifty good workers could roll by hand. Allen & Ginter turned the machine down, but Buck Duke immediately saw its potential. He had the Bonsack machine running smoothly in his Durham plant by 1884.

The trouble with churning out so many thousands of cigarettes, though, was that Duke somehow had to make enough people want to buy them. At the time most people thought cigarettes were for sissies. Duke launched an aggressive advertising campaign that foreshadowed the lavish promotions cigarette makers would use for decades to come.

He moved to New York, opened a small factory there, and splashed the Duke name on walls, bill-boards, and newspaper pages. His cigarettes were put in bright packaging with striking symbols and catchy names. Duke gathered celebrity endorse-ments for his cigarettes and used pictures of attrac-tive women in his ads. The company sponsored a roller-skating team it named the Cross Cuts, after one of Duke's cigarette brands. Free samples of Cross Cut cigarettes were handed out at games when the team went on tour. The gimmick won Duke free publicity in newspapers across the country, and Cross Cut sales soared.

Duke brought sacks of his cigarettes to New York's immigrant station, giving samples to every male immigrant he met. He intended for these newcomers to help spread the word all over the United States. The marketing tactics of the former North Carolina farm boy worked spectacularly. By 1889, five years after his move to New York, Duke made and sold about half of the 2.1 billion cigarettes consumed in the nation. His competitors were hurting, as Duke had planned. His business strategy was simple: Dominate the market, then force rivals out of business or buy them out.

The strategy cost Duke an enormous amount of money. But he came up with an idea to bring his rivals under his control while making it possible for all to profit again. In 1889, Duke met with the leaders of competing firms and formed the American Tobacco Company, a "trust" in which the member firms would work together to set prices and control the sale of cigarettes. Duke was made president of the new cooperative. Creation of the trust put 90 percent of the tobacco market under Duke's control. He then set out to get rid of his remaining competitors and eventually bought or drove out of business about 250 small tobacco companies.

But the American public had already seen what trusts could do. Similar trusts had been formed in the railroad, petroleum, sugar, copper, lumber, and other industries. By cooperating with each other, giant corporations could force consumers to pay higher prices for goods. At the public's demand, the federal government tried to rein in the power of big corporations by passing the Sherman Antitrust Act in 1890, the same year Buck Duke officially incorporated his American Tobacco Company.

For a time, the tobacco trust kept growing. Having taken over cigarette manufacturing in the United States, Duke further enlarged his empire by gobbling up firms that produced chewing tobacco. The biggest of these included Liggett & Myers and P. Lorillard—two names that would survive and thrive in the twentieth-century heyday of the tobacco industry. By 1900, Duke had bought up these major companies; smaller firms he pushed into bankruptcy. Among the firms that vanished was his first rival, Durham Tobacco Company, the producer of Bull Durham. In the same voracious way, Duke assembled a concern that controlled 80 percent of the nation's snuff production. The trust formed smaller monopolies, still under trust control, to make other products needed in tobacco production and sale, such as flavorings and packaging materials. Finally, Duke went after an old North Carolina rival: Richard J. Reynolds. Reynolds sold control of his tobacco company to Duke, but he continued running it and used trust money to buy up a number of his small competitors.

Duke set out to take control of the tobacco industry in Great Britain as he had in the United States but found he could not bully his competitors there into submission. Instead, he reached an agreement with them that in 1902 created the first global trust, British-American Tobacco Company, or BAT. Duke made himself president of that trust, too. Soon, BAT built factories in Shanghai and other places, bringing Bright Leaf tobacco cigarettes to even remote corners of Asia.

While the tobacco trust grew in power and wealth, opposition to it also grew. Moralists claimed that cigarettes, so easy to buy and use, would prove irresistible to boys and would lead them into lives of depravity and crime. Tobacco opponents formed the National Anti-Cigarette League. Cigarette sales were outlawed in Iowa, North Dakota, and Tennessee by 1900, and in 1901 twelve other states considered a ban.

Farmers, too, raised their voices in protest. The trust had long squeezed them by forcing them to sell their crop at ruinously low prices. In 1904, North Carolina farmers tried to organize their resistance; the trust quickly broke up the farmers' cooperative by offering a few growers slightly higher prices. Kentucky farmers fought back more stubbornly, threatening any who thought to break ranks. In December 1906 protesters burned down two American Tobacco Company warehouses, destroying 300,000 pounds (136,200 kilograms) of tobacco.

The U.S. government, barraged with demands that it enforce its own antitrust law, finally took action. In 1907, President Theodore Roosevelt launched the government's prosecution of the American Tobacco Company. Duke and his team of attorneys contended that the firm had done nothing wrong and

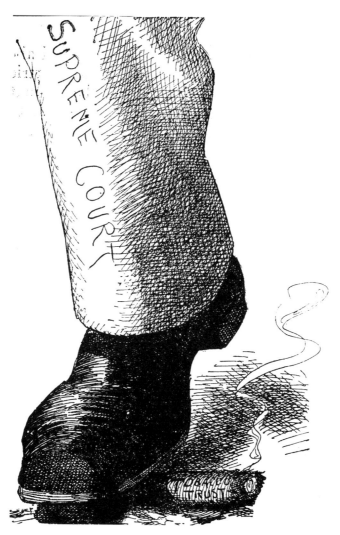

By 1911 the Supreme Court broke up the tobacco trust, based not on the moralists' objections to the enlistment of young people as smokers, nor on the farmers' complaints about being unfairly squeezed—but because of the illegal competitive practices that the monopoly engendered.

had merely succeeded at what every business tried to do: make money. Testifying coolly, Duke declared: "I never bought any business with the idea of eliminating competition; it was always the idea of an investment."[2]

In 1911 the case reached the Supreme Court, which ruled that American Tobacco was an illegal trust and had set out to destroy competitors and take control of the market. The court ordered Duke to break up the monopoly.

Duke's plan created several firms that kept some old names. The biggest were American Tobacco, Liggett & Myers, and P. Lorillard. Smaller spin-offs included R. J. Reynolds Company, and British-American Tobacco. Together, these firms would define the American tobacco industry for much of the twentieth century.

Chapter Three
"BLOW SOME MY WAY"

The breakup of the trust, far from dooming the cigarette makers, was followed by an explosion in profits. Over the next five decades, cigarettes would become symbols of maturity, independence, glamour, and a host of other qualities that smokers wanted to communicate about themselves. Ironically, during the same period, scientists would produce strong evidence that cigarettes harmed smokers' health—evidence the public would for years scarcely seem to notice.

When the tobacco trust was dissolved, Richard J. Reynolds took immediate advantage of his new independence. He turned his firm, RJR, toward a product the company had not made before: cigarettes. Reynolds made two decisions that would change the American cigarette industry. First, he chose to pour company resources into promoting a single brand, a marketing strategy no other firm had used. Second, Reynolds tried a new blend of tobaccos, combining Bright, Burley, and a bit of Turkish leaf. He called his brand Camel.

It happened that the Barnum and Bailey circus visited RJR's headquarters city, Winston-Salem, in the fall of 1913, when Reynolds needed an illustration for the Camel package. There, among the circus menagerie, was the perfect model—a dromedary named Old Joe. Camel was launched with heavy advertising in mid-1914 and quickly became popular. When Richard J. Reynolds died in 1918, his Camels commanded about 40 percent of the nation's cigarette sales.

R. J. Reynolds owns the rights to a charming photograph of a circus dromedary, the original "Old Joe." As an indication of the sensitive political climate surrounding tobacco and youth, we were unable to obtain permission from the tobacco company to reproduce the photo because this book is intended for readers under age twenty-three.

At American Tobacco, meanwhile, Buck Duke had retired. (In his remaining years, he would found an electric company and give enough money to a small college to enable it to grow into the prestigious Duke University.) Duke's successors at American Tobacco fought back against RJR's Camel with a new brand of their own called Lucky Strike. Advertised with the meaningless slogan "It's Toasted," Lucky Strikes debuted in 1916.

An advertising war erupted. Lucky's lively promotion included the new technique of skywriting. In 1921, RJR bandied its new slogan "I'd Walk a Mile for a Camel" in publications and across billboards all over the country. Liggett & Myers jumped into the contest, too, successfully pushing its Chesterfield brand with the slogan "They Satisfy." Throughout the 1920s, 1930s, and 1940s, the three brands would dominate the U.S. cigarette market.

But slick advertising wasn't all the tobacco companies had on their side. Changes in American society during the first quarter of the twentieth century also helped them.

Cigarettes had been regarded as something for sissies and rich college boys. World War I (1914–1918) changed that. Soldiers took cigarettes into combat as a convenient source of quick relaxation, and the Red Cross and YMCA worked to see that soldiers had enough cigarettes along with their food rations. Suddenly, the connection with all-American warriors made cigarettes a symbol of toughness and masculinity. At the same time on the homefront, women fought for greater rights. Shortly after World War I

*If the primitive graphics do not convince you that
this is one of the very first Camel ads, from around 1920,
then look at the price: 20 for 10 cents!*

it's toasted
·· your throat protection

Exactly what toasting had to do with "throat protection" is unclear, but apparently the ads were effective, as "Luckies" became one of the top three brands in the United States.

ended, American women won the right to vote. Women had smoked privately for some time, but now they began to smoke openly as a way to express their new sense of equality.

Although cigarette makers wanted more women customers, they courted them cautiously because public smoking by women was frowned on. RJR commissioned oil paintings for its Camel ads in the 1920s, showing elegant settings in which men smoked but women only watched. Philip Morris, a tiny company at the time, took a bolder approach. It introduced a women's cigarette called Marlboro and advertised the brand with a picture of a female hand holding a cigarette and the slogan "Mild as May." American Tobacco capitalized on the fact that smoking suppressed appetite, urging women who wanted to stay slender to "Reach for a Lucky instead of a sweet." Pilot Amelia Earhart and singer Al Jolson appeared in some of these ads with thinness themes. The clear message: Smoking cigarettes is for glamorous, beautiful people.

The evolution of Liggett & Myers's Chesterfield ads illustrates the changes in attitude. Magazine advertisements in the 1920s centered on themes of victory, patriotism, romance, and elegance. Even ads that featured strong, independent-looking women did not show them as smokers. One late-1920s Chesterfield ad shows a man and a woman in a romantic, moonlit setting—he's smoking, she's not—with the woman asking her companion to "Blow some my way." A 1931 ad pictures a woman looking thoughtful, with text that says she doesn't smoke but her girlfriends have told her how great Chesterfields are. Finally, in 1932, three women are shown enjoying cigarettes, while the ad text exults: "Three more Chesterfield smokers!"

Smoking became a sign of sophistication and confidence for women. With the return of the American soldiers who had started smoking in the trenches and the addition of so many women smokers, per capita consumption of tobacco doubled between 1920 and 1930.

The U.S. government recognized a good potential source of revenue in tobacco. Rather than trying to ban cigarettes as it had tried to ban alcohol, the national government in the 1920s raised its taxes on cigarettes. Iowa, which had outlawed cigarettes only two decades earlier, in 1921 became the first state to tax them. Other states followed, and by 1927 all remaining state bans on cigarette sales had been abandoned. U.S. tax revenue from all tobacco products had been $58 million in 1910; in 1930, it was about ten times that much, most of it from cigarettes.

The 1920s also saw growth of a more ominous kind. The diagnosis of lung cancer, formerly a rare disease, became more common. But the number of lung cancer deaths was still very small compared with the number of deaths caused by the era's big killers, influenza and tuberculosis. Furthermore, some people theorized that lung cancer itself was not becoming more common, but that the diagnosis was turning up more frequently because doctors could now spot the cancer by using X-ray machines. Some researchers noted a pattern among lung cancer patients that seemed to link the disease to smoking.

Although the smoking public didn't seem to be troubled by these developments, people did notice that smoking irritated their throats and made them cough. Cigarette makers responded with claims of "mildness" and new slogans. Ads for P. Lorillard's new brand, Old Gold, promised: "Not a Cough in a Carload." RJR assured smokers: "Not a Single Case of Throat Irritation Due to Smoking Camels." American Tobacco offered doctors five free cartons of Luckies in exchange for their endorsements and then claimed: "20,679 Physicians Say Luckies Are Less Irritating."

The Great Depression during the 1930s brought changes in the cigarette industry. A fierce price war enabled the small firms of Brown & Williamson and

A 1932 Lucky Strike ad still boasted "It's toasted"
—but with a few additions. The brand now implicitly
claims that smoking is glamorous and it's for women,
and explicitly declares that it protects the throat
against irritation and coughs.

VOICES . . . OF SALESMANSHIP

"Chesterfields hit the smoke-spot. They let you know you are smoking—they 'SATISFY'! Yet, they're MILD!"

> *September 15, 1917, ad in*
> Collier's Weekly *magazine,*
> *with images of well-dressed men*

"Ready for most anything, just having a good time swinging and smoking. Well yes, Chesterfield—they satisfy."

> *1933 magazine ad, with picture of a woman*
> *riding on a swing, cigarette in hand*

"Be happy, go Lucky.
Be happy, go Lucky Strike.
Be happy, go Lucky.
Go Lucky Strike today."

> *TV commercial jingle, "Your Hit Parade,"*
> *March 1952*

"I like good anything—good fun, good smoking. Naturally, I smoke Luckies. To put it poetically:
    I hope I'm not a crank,
    But I've got one foible.
    I don't enjoy anything
    unless it's enjoyable.
    I'm pernickety about what I like,
    and for 30 years, I've smoked Lucky Strike."

> *Ogden Nash, shown sitting and smoking,*
> *in a TV commercial during*
> *"Your Hit Parade," April 1954*

Philip Morris to grow, taking customers away from the four biggest manufacturers–American Tobacco, RJR, P. Lorillard, and Liggett & Myers. The firms' competition to win customers by trimming prices inevitably ended up cutting the income of the people at the foundation of this profitable pyramid: the to-bacco growers. By 1933 many tobacco farmers lived in poverty. Desperate, the growers asked the federal government for help.

The result was the Agricultural Adjustment Act, a system to keep tobacco prices at a level that would let farmers make a living. It functioned this way: The cigarette makers agreed to tell the federal govern-ment how much tobacco they expected to buy the next year. The Agriculture Department could then tell each grower how many acres of tobacco (later changed to pounds) he would be allowed to grow. Farmers agreed to accept these limits, or "quotas," on their crop, and the government agreed to buy any leaf the cigarette companies didn't buy, at a price set before the growing season began. The system worked. By 1936 leaf prices paid to farmers had doubled from a few years earlier. With some minor changes, the system would remain in place for at least six decades.

In that era before television, movies were the most important entertainment medium. It was the midst of the Great Depression, and many Americans were unemployed. So in movies of the 1930s, gangsters and blue-collar workers smoked. At a time when wealthy, high-living people were widely regarded with resentment, the cigarette-smoking characters were considered heroes. Cigars, by contrast, were shown as being favored by fat, arrogant, wealthy men, the kind who took advantage of good hardworking people.

Meanwhile, cigarette companies made increasingly brash claims that they were looking out for smokers' health. RJR promised in its Camel ads, "They don't get your wind," with endorsements by celebrity athletes. Testimonials from society women accompanied the ad slogan "For Digestion's Sake–Smoke Camels." The American Tobacco Company made Lucky the sponsor of radio programs, notably the Lucky Strike "Your Hit Parade" that played the most popular tunes every week. To reach listeners of other tastes, Lucky sponsored broadcasts from the New York Metropolitan Opera and a talk show with intellectual leaders of the day. ATC refined and embellished its endorsement technique, claiming with immense exaggeration that it had "sworn records" showing that thousands of tobacco experts agreed Lucky had the best tobacco.

The smaller firms came out with innovations that gave the appearance of addressing health concerns. Brown & Williamson in 1933 introduced a menthol-flavored brand called Kool with the slogan "Give Your Throat a Kool Vacation!" Menthol, a peppermint plant extract, slightly numbed the throat; the smoke was no less toxic, but a smoker would feel less throat irritation. Three years later B&W brought out Viceroy, which featured a filter that was supposed to reduce throat irritation. The 1930s saw the appearance of other new gimmicks, including king-size and economy brands.

The still-small Philip Morris Company revived the old brand name Philip Morris with a new tobacco blend and put it in a package that implied, falsely, that it was a fancy English cigarette. The brand debuted in 1933; soon its radio ads and their high-pitched cry of "Call for Philip Morris!" became familiar to listeners across the country. Philip Morris ads boldly—and deceptively—claimed "eminent medical authorities" believed a new chemical in the cigarettes cured throat irritation. By 1938, Philip Morris was the fourth-biggest-selling brand.

Almost as if in another universe, research into the serious health consequences of smoking gained steam at the same time. Some scientists suspected it was not nicotine but the chemicals produced by burning tobacco that were somehow connected to cancer. A researcher in Argentina discovered a way to distill the tarry residue from tobacco smoke and remove the nicotine from it. When he applied the distillate to the ears of rabbits, tumors grew.

Warnings came from a number of corners. The magazine *Consumer Reports* in 1938 conducted the first of what would become regular tests of cigarette ad claims regarding nicotine content; the tests showed Chesterfield and Marlboro to be the strongest. In the same year a Johns Hopkins University researcher found that smokers generally died younger. In 1939 a New Orleans surgeon put forth the idea that it took perhaps twenty years or more for smoking to produce cancer. A German researcher that year made the connection between a current surge in lung cancer cases and the fact that men had started smoking

People under thirty will no doubt find this 1946 Camel ad unbelievable—but cigarette companies competed in claiming the greatest health benefits back then, and it was common practice to use medical endorsements to counteract the dawning public suspicion about the risks of smoking.

cigarettes in huge numbers during World War I. Further, he found that the disease was six times more common in men than in women. A year later Mayo Clinic researchers reported on the first study to link smoking to heart disease.

These were voices in the wilderness. The public didn't hear the alarm, and even many physicians dismissed it. The widely read magazine *Reader's Digest* tried to call public attention to the case against tobacco with a 1941 article titled "Nicotine Knockout." That year, however, the United States entered World War II and a new generation of young American men learned to rely on their little sticks of tobacco for comfort in the trenches. The 12 million American soldiers in the war smoked an average of 30 cigarettes a day each. They handed out cigarettes to the people they liberated as a gesture of goodwill. President Roosevelt declared tobacco to be one of the nation's essential materials in wartime. Women, moving into high-pressure manufacturing jobs while men were away fighting, smoked more, too.

The federal government, which had not tried to control cigarette makers since the breakup of the tobacco trust, made two attempts to regulate the industry in the early 1940s. The first, an antitrust suit, ended only in small fines. In the government's second attack, the Federal Trade Commission filed actions against the firms for making deceptive advertising claims. But in a tactic they would practice throughout the rest of the twentieth century, the tobacco companies sent their lawyers to file endless motions and appeals; the case dragged on for thirteen years.

One popular New York City sight for visiting children was the Camel ad in which a smoker blew smoke rings out over delighted crowds in Times Square.

All the while, cigarette makers kept up their battle for the hearts, lungs, and dollars of Americans. RJR in 1942 put up in New York's Times Square a billboard that was two stories high and half a block wide. It sported the slogan "I'd Walk a Mile for a Camel," along with a picture of an American military man that blew real smoke rings. A Camel magazine ad showed a pilot with a cigarette in his lips and the words "You Want Steady Nerves When You're Flying Uncle Sam's Bombers Across the Ocean." American Tobacco hammered its "Lucky Strike Means Fine Tobacco" into the public consciousness, so much so that before long the slogan was reduced to the abbreviation "L.S./M.F.T." Philip Morris leaped into the new medium of television by sponsoring "Candid Camera" and "This Is Your Life."

With the end of the Depression and the return of prosperity, moviemakers again put cigarettes in the hands of glamorous characters. In films of the 1940s, it was not unusual for virtually everyone to smoke. By the way they handled their cigarettes, actors could show tension, fear, triumph, relief, and a whole range of emotions and relationships.

From the farmer who grew the golden leaf to the retailer who watched cigarettes fly off his store shelves, all parts of the tobacco industry saw profits balloon in the 1940s as Americans smoked more and more. By the end of that decade, studies showed that more than half of males over age eighteen and about a third of females smoked cigarettes.

But the industry was about to take its first serious punch from health researchers, a hit that would send American smokers reeling as well.

Chapter Four

"CAUTION: CIGARETTE SMOKING MAY BE HAZARDOUS ..."

The first major studies indicting smoking as a threat to health appeared in the early 1950s. At least a few American smokers heard the alarm and heeded it. For the first time, smokers began cutting down or quitting. But it would take almost half a century for health advocates, politicians, and the public to muster a powerful enough attack to put cigarette makers on the defensive. Until the early 1990s, it looked as if Big Tobacco simply could not be reined in.

Several landmark research efforts marked the beginning of the new surge in health concerns. A New York scientist reported in 1950 on a study that showed hospital patients who smoked a pack of cigarettes a day were ten times as likely to develop lung cancer as nonsmokers. Another study, published the same year, found that 96.5 percent of lung cancer patients were at least moderately heavy smokers. A third study around the same time indicated that people who smoked fifty or more cigarettes a day were fifty times as likely as nonsmokers to get lung cancer. And in a famous study a few years later, a researcher distilled the gas and particles from cigarette smoke into a liquid; when he painted this liquid onto the shaved backs of laboratory mice, tumors grew.[1]

The tobacco industry immediately scoffed at the studies. Then tobacco company leaders met and made a strategy decision that would set their path for the next forty years. Instead of seeking the help of scientists and doctors in addressing the frightening studies, they turned to public-relations people for advice.

As a result, in January 1954 the companies took out full-page ads headlined "A Frank Statement to Cigarette Smokers" in more than four hundred newspapers. The ads announced the companies' joint creation of an agency they called the Tobacco Industry Research Committee (TIRC, later to be renamed the Council for Tobacco Research). The industry promised that its new committee would support research to use "every scientific means . . . to get all the facts as soon as possible."[2] In reality, though, over the years the "research committee" would steer grant money to studies that had little to do with smoking, yank funding from projects that produced data the industry didn't like, and pump out publicity material denying there was any danger in cigarettes. Its true mission was to keep alive the fiction that there was a continuing "controversy" over the hazards of smoking.

The head of Philip Morris told company stockholders in 1954 that the health studies had to be taken seriously—not because of the peril to smokers, but because of the threat to company profits. Meanwhile, he assured the rest of the country: "If the industry leaders really believed that cigarettes cause cancer, they would stop making them."[3] When a massive American Cancer Society study in the mid-fifties showed that smokers died younger than nonsmokers and for the first time linked smoking to heart disease, the TIRC issued a statement that would remain the industry's standard response, saying there was "no conclusive scientific evidence" that cigarettes harmed people. (Decades later, documents from inside cigarette companies would show that tobacco executives did believe in the 1950s that cigarettes contained substances that caused cancer.)

At mid-century almost half the adults in the United States smoked cigarettes, and it was clear some were worried. While evidence continued to emerge from laboratories, and while the cancer death rate doubled in a decade, cigarette companies met public concern by developing filter tips. They promoted this new technology with ads that boasted, "Here's How Science Solved Your Problem of Sensitivity to Nicotine and Tars" and "Just What the Doctor Ordered!" The companies also started trying to outdo each other with claims of low tar and nicotine.

The substance known as "tar" is actually made up of microscopic particles of hundreds of chemical compounds produced by the burning of the tobacco and additives in cigarettes. These compounds include phenol, naphthalene, and the heavy metal cadmium. Cigarette smoke also contains toxic gases, including carbon monoxide, nitrogen oxide, ammonia, form-aldehyde, benzene, and hydrogen cyanide, among others. More than 4,700 chemicals have been identi-fied in cigarette smoke; more than 40 of those are known to cause cancer.

Nicotine, the addictive agent in smoke, is a poi-son sometimes used in pesticides. It is an oily liquid alkaloid with an acrid taste. Although a single drop of pure nicotine would kill an average-size man, the amount in a puff of cigarette smoke is small enough for the body to quickly break down. When cigarette smoke is inhaled, it is rapidly absorbed through the lungs into the bloodstream. Within seven seconds, nicotine reaches the brain; in fifteen to twenty sec-onds, it reaches all parts of the body.

The drug affects the body in ways that mystified researchers for some time. People smoke to keep themselves alert, but also to calm themselves–how could the same chemical bring both of these effects? Scientists discovered that nicotine has a two-phase action. With the first hit, the smoker's heartbeat quick-ens, blood vessels constrict, blood pressure jumps, and skin cools. The body feels a surge of energy, something like the adrenaline fight-or-flight response. Larger doses, though, block that same response. The heart slows down, in turn slowing the delivery of oxygen to the brain, and the nicotine then acts as a sedative. Nicotine also accounts for the fact that to-bacco suppresses appetite: It lowers the blood's in-sulin level, reducing the craving for sweets, and at the same time speeds up the rate at which the body burns fuel. And as for the cigarette companies' claims

A Wicks cartoon pokes fun at the tobacco industry's claim that nicotine was not addictive. Note the trembling of the mice—a symptom now proven to be one of many associated with nicotine withdrawal.

that they had lowered nicotine levels, studies have shown that smokers' bodies aren't fooled. Smokers of low-nicotine cigarettes tend to draw more deeply, hold the smoke in their lungs longer, smoke more cigarettes, and smoke each one farther down to get the amount of nicotine they crave.

When the federal government started to show concern about the dangers of smoking in the late 1950s, the cigarette companies augmented the work of the TIRC by establishing the Tobacco Institute, whose purposes were to do public relations and lobby, or try to influence lawmakers, on behalf of the industry. It managed, through skillful lobbying and carefully placed campaign contributions, to keep cigarette taxes from rising and tobacco from being officially declared a hazardous substance.

In the early 1960s the American Cancer Society and other large health organizations applied some pressure of their own on the government. The result was a report that would begin an eventual turnaround in public sentiment. For more than a year, a panel of scientists called the Surgeon General's Advisory Committee reviewed the thousands of studies that had already been done on how smoking affected health. In 1964 the surgeon general (the nation's highest medical official) presented the committee's findings to the American people: Cigarette smoking caused cancer and was "a health hazard of sufficient importance in the United States to warrant appropriate remedial action."[4] The only "remedial action" Congress took right away was to pass a law in 1965 that cigarette packs had to carry a label that said: "Caution: Cigarette Smoking May Be Hazardous to Your Health." The law also called for the surgeon general to report to Congress once a year on the latest research on smoking and health.

Other federal government actions followed. In 1968 broadcasters were required to give free airtime for antismoking public-service announcements to counter the enticing images in cigarette commercials. The next year cigarette makers were required to toughen the package warning labels to read: "Warning: The Surgeon General has determined that cigarette smoking is dangerous to your health and may cause lung cancer and other diseases." In 1971, TV advertising of cigarettes was banned, but the required warning label was toned down to say only that cigarette smoking "is dangerous to your health." Commercial airlines were ordered to have nonsmoking sections on all flights starting in 1972; eighteen years later, the government banned all smoking on flights within the United States. In 1984, Congress mandated four new label warnings: "Cigarette Smoke Contains Carbon Monoxide"; "Smoking Causes Lung Cancer, Heart Disease, Emphysema, and May Complicate Pregnancy"; "Smoking by Pregnant Women May Result in Fetal Injury, Premature Birth and Low Birth Weight"; and "Quitting Smoking Now Greatly Reduces Serious Risks to Your Health."

Over the same three and a half decades, the annual surgeon general's reports dealt powerfully with the role of smoking in heart disease and emphysema, the danger of environmental tobacco smoke (ETS) to nonsmokers, the effects a pregnant woman's smoking have on her fetus, nicotine addiction, tobacco use by young people, and smoking among ethnic minorities. Cigarette company executives kept up their denials, but the American public took the reports seriously. About 42 percent of American adults smoked cigarettes when the first surgeon general's report was issued. In the mid-seventies, that rate began to fall; by 1995, fewer than one in four adults smoked.

*A somewhat poignant reminder that the teens of
the 1960s, like all teens, considered themselves
invulnerable to health problems. The warning labels on
cigarette packs were not enough, and it took an entire
generation of antismoking programs, many administered
through the educational system, to get a significant
number of young people to take the warnings seriously.*

VOICE . . . OF EXPERIENCE

"Between fourteen and fifteen years old, I started trying my first cigarettes. By the time I was eighteen, I was certainly hooked....

"I stopped after I contracted throat cancer and cancer of the larynx.... I knew my larynx was going to be removed, and I knew I would wind up with the valve through which I breathe in my neck.... I don't reckon you can picture the havoc it wreaks until you see yourself in the mirror for the first time. I was white and pale. I had all these stitches in my neck. I had a hole right in the base of my throat. Tubes through my nose. I had a feeding tube. There was a stainless steel pipe inside this stoma [a permanent opening in his throat]. I had basically been opened up from under my chin all the way down to the top of my breastbone....

"If I had not contracted this throat cancer, I would be smoking right this minute. I thought my life revolved around it. I got up in the morning, I had to have a cigarette to get my day started. If I had breakfast or coffee, I had to have one or two cigarettes. I had to have a cigarette to drive to work. I had to have a cigarette the first time I could take a break at work. At the time, I did not liken that to getting my next fix. But my body was telling me, 'Time for another jolt, go get another smoke, two if you're lucky.' I lived that way for thirty-plus years.

"As long as I could get me a cigarette, then I was ready to tackle the world."

Wade Hampton, age fifty-one, of Norwood, North Carolina, former smoker who had to have his voice box removed after he was diagnosed with cancer in 1994. October 28, 1998

Meanwhile, nonsmokers gradually lost patience. In workplaces, on public transportation, in places where people shopped, dined, or conducted business, cigarette smoke filled the air. While tobacco companies had proclaimed that everyone should have the right to smoke if they chose, more and more Americans began to insist that nonsmokers were also entitled to a choice: to breathe smoke-free air. Small antismoking groups sprang up, eventually giving rise to national organizations with names such as Action on Smoking and Health and Americans for Non-smokers' Rights. The surgeon general's reports gave fuel to the nonsmokers' rights movement, especially the 1986 edition that said ETS, or "secondhand" smoke, can cause lung cancer. The federal Environmental Protection Agency (EPA) backed up that assertion in 1993, explaining that secondhand smoke contained, among other carcinogens, the radioactive polonium-210.

The movement had its effect. Beginning in the 1970s, states and cities enacted laws that prohibited smoking in various public places. A growing number of employers experimented with smoking and nonsmoking areas, often finding that the only way to keep any area smoke free was to make the entire workplace smoke free. Hotels, restaurants, and other private businesses heeded the wishes of their non-smoking customers as well.

A new trend emerged in the 1990s: a rise in cigar smoking. Between 1993 and 1996, cigar smoking increased by about half and seemed likely to continue gaining popularity. The practice was lent a glamor-

A Kirk cartoon expresses American society's attitude toward smokers. Lepers, in biblical times, were considered social outcasts and were forced to live in isolated colonies because of the unsightliness and possible contagious nature of their disease. Here a colony of lepers is shown looking down on a colony of smokers.

ous air by celebrities who made a show of smoking cigars, and restaurants and nightclubs began to open cigar-smoking sections. Cigar smoke is not generally drawn deep into the lungs, as cigarette smoke is. But cigars carry most of the same cancer-causing chemicals as cigarettes.

Some people have turned to smokeless tobacco for their nicotine fix. Smokeless tobacco is called plug, leaf, or snuff; anyone who watches baseball games on TV has seen professional players spitting the juice of their chewing tobacco. Of particular concern to researchers is "dipping snuff," a moist powder of tobacco that is placed between the cheek and gum. Even though snuff does not send smoke into the lungs, its nicotine and carcinogens are absorbed in the mouth. Thus, while it may be less annoying to other people, it still endangers the health of the person using it.

The statistics that had accumulated by the end of the twentieth century were staggering:

- Each year more than 400,000 Americans die from smoking-related illnesses. That's one death in five in the United States— more deaths than are caused by car accidents, AIDS, heroin, cocaine, alcohol, suicide, and murder combined; about as many Americans as died in battle in World War I, World War II, the Korean War, and the Vietnam War combined. Globally the annual death toll from smoking is about three million; it is expected to hit ten million by 2025.
- About one fourth of cigarette smokers die from smoking-related illnesses.
- Smoking is responsible for more than 85 percent of lung cancers, about 30 percent of all cancer deaths, and almost 20 percent of deaths from heart disease. Since 1987 lung cancer has killed more women

each year than breast cancer. Smokers are eleven times as likely to die from lung cancer as are nonsmokers.

- Cigarette smoke is also linked to cancers of the kidney, bladder, cervix, pancreas, mouth, throat, and esophagus.
- Smoking cuts an average of seven years off a smoker's life.
- Every year about 3,000 nonsmokers die of lung cancer, and about 35,000 nonsmokers die of heart disease from breathing others' cigarette smoke. Children of smoking parents have more ear infections and respiratory ailments than children in smoke-free homes.
- One pregnant woman in four smokes. Pregnant women who smoke are more likely to deliver prematurely, to miscarry, or to have stillborn children. Their babies weigh an average of 6 ounces (170 grams) less at birth than the babies of nonsmokers; lower birth weight makes a baby more vulnerable to health problems and more likely to die during infancy. Their babies' risk of Sudden Infant Death Syndrome is tripled.
- Nicotine kills brain cells and retards brain development in human fetuses. The child of a woman who smoked during pregnancy is more likely to have learning disabilities, attention deficit disorder, hyperactivity, or mental retardation. Pregnant

smokers pass a powerful carcinogen called NNK to their fetuses.

- Smoking is a major cause of death and illness among American minority groups. African-American men die of lung cancer at a rate about 50 percent higher than that of white men. A 1998 study suggested that blacks absorb more nicotine per cigarette than smokers of other ethnicities.

- Cigar smokers have a cancer death rate about 34 percent higher than that of non-smokers. They have between four and ten times as great a risk of dying from cancers of the mouth, larynx, or esophagus.

- Snuff dippers have several times as high a risk of oral cancer as people who don't use tobacco. With long-term use, that risk may be fifty times as high as a nonuser's. While only about 4 percent of adult men use smokeless tobacco, between 10 percent and 20 percent of male high school students use it.

- When a cigarette smoker quits, the body begins healing itself within twenty minutes. After five years, the risk of death by lung cancer drops by half; after fifteen years, the lung cancer death risk is only slightly higher than that of a lifelong nonsmoker, and the risk of heart disease is the same as a nonsmoker's. The destruction of lung tissue that leads to emphysema, however, is permanent.

- Four fifths of smokers say they would not start smoking if they had it to do over. But 90 percent of smokers who try to quit fail.[5]

Tobacco has claimed the lives of some of America's most talented and admired citizens.

Journalist Edward R. Murrow interviewed movie stars Humphrey Bogart and Lauren Bacall on his TV show in 1954. Both men smoked throughout the interview; both later died of lung cancer. Evarts Graham, coauthor of one of the seminal 1950 smoking studies, had been a heavy smoker but quit after he saw his study's results. He died of lung cancer in 1957. Baseball great Babe Ruth chewed tobacco, as do many players today. He died of throat cancer.

Musician George Harrison, a former member of the Beatles, was diagnosed with throat cancer in 1997, but his story appeared to have a happier outcome. In June 1998, Harrison announced that he had beaten the disease. And he told the world where it had come from: "I got it purely from smoking."[6]

Chapter Five

THE THIRTEEN-MONTH CROP

The industry that grosses about $50 billion a year in the United States begins with a plant that grows from a dust-size seed and is traditionally said to demand a farmer's attention for thirteen months before it is ready to harvest.

Tobacco, a botanical relative of potatoes, peppers, eggplant, and deadly nightshade, originated in the Western Hemisphere. About eight thousand years ago, native peoples dispersed it throughout the Americas. Although many species existed, the only two that were farmed were those later named *Nicotiana rustica* and *Nicotiana tabacum. N. rustica* was grown in a variety of environments, but *N. tabacum,* the ancestor of today's commercial tobacco, was best suited for growing in tropical climates.

The main tobacco in American cigarettes is the Bright Leaf variety that was discovered in North Carolina in 1839. It is sometimes called Virginia or, more commonly, flue-cured. Bright tobacco favors sandy, loamy, slightly acidic soil and hot, moist days and nights–all of which it finds in the southeastern United States. Most of the nation's Bright tobacco is raised in North Carolina; it is also grown in four other states. Because of its combination of soil, climate, and experience, the United States has long been recognized as the source of the world's best flue-cured tobacco. The other chief tobacco in cigarettes is White Burley, or simply Burley, which was mostly used for chewing before R. J. Reynolds blended it into Camels. It thrives in the rich, dark soil of Kentucky and Tennessee; half a dozen other states have small Burley crops. Another tobacco, called Maryland and grown in Maryland and Pennsylvania, is used in small amounts in cigarettes. Cigar tobacco is farmed in several northern states.

Tobacco seed is so small that 1 ounce (28 grams) of it contains about 300,000 seeds; that ounce of seed will produce 6 acres (2.4 hectares) of tobacco, or about 13,000 pounds (5,902 kilograms) of leaf. Until recently, tobacco was cultivated by methods that had changed little since colonial times. Traditionally, in late winter, the grower broadcast seeds onto beds that had been carefully prepared to be free of weeds and pests. The ideal seedbed sloped slightly to the south, to catch the best morning sunshine. There, the seeds would germinate and the plants grow for two to three months. During that time, the farmer would need to check the seedlings every day for insects and disease, and also prepare the fields in which the tobacco plants would mature—1 acre (0.4 hectare) for every 100 square yards (84 square meters) of seedbed.

In the old days, transplanting the seedlings was tedious work. The farmer and whatever family members he trusted to do the job right would pluck the seedlings from their bed in spring and haul them to the field, where rows of mounded soil waited. With a wooden peg about 8 inches (20 centimeters) long and 1.5 inches (3.8 centimeters) in diameter, the farmer would make a hole in the soil, stand a tiny plant in it, push dirt back around the roots, then gently pour on a ladleful of water.

Tobacco demands close attention throughout its growing season. The five thousand or so plants on each acre have to be weeded at least weekly. Before pesticides, destructive pests such as the fat green hornworm had to be picked off by hand. Crop rotation has long been one of the farmer's chief weapons in controlling bugs and diseases, but the alternate crops need to be selected carefully because they affect the soil composition.

Today, many tobacco farmers start their seedlings in greenhouses and use gas fumigants to kill off diseases and pests hiding in the soil. Machines pulled by tractors make transplanting much easier. When the tobacco plant's single stalk flowers, the farmer snaps off the tip, just as Native Americans did in pre-Columbian times. This "topping" forces growth into the roots and leaves but encourages new sprouts or "suckers" to grow at the base of the leaves. Suckers, if they are allowed to develop, have to be removed by hand to let the leaves on the main stalk grow. Farmers today often prevent suckers by applying a growth-retardant chemical when the plants are topped.

While the plants are in the field, the grower has to keep close track of the soil acidity and moisture and see to it that the plants get the proper nutrients. Tobacco can thrive in ground that would be good for growing little else, but the plant is sensitive to differences in soil, climate, and farming practices. Many pests, fungi, and viral as well as bacterial infections can menace the crop. When the tobacco plant is fully grown, it is nearly as tall as a man, with a stalk as thick as his wrist, and yields about twenty leaves that are up to 30 inches (76 centimeters) long.

Nicotine doesn't exist in the seed but begins forming in the root of the tobacco plant within days after germination and then is stored in the leaves. Nicotine content can be affected by many factors, such as:

- The level of nitrogen fertility. Nitrogen is part of the nicotine molecule; more nitrogen in the soil means more nicotine in the leaves.
- Root health. Diseases and parasites can interfere with nicotine synthesis.
- The spacing of plants. The closer they are, the less nicotine.
- Early topping and vigilant sucker control, which increase nicotine.
- Soil moisture. Low moisture slows growth and increases nicotine in the leaves.
- Stalk position. In Bright tobacco, nicotine

increases as you move up the plant; Burley leaves from the middle of the plant up have about the same level of nicotine.

Bright, or flue-cured, and Burley tobaccos differ in their chemical composition, and so are used differently. Flue-cured is higher in sugar, lighter in the "flavor" of its smoke, and lower in nicotine; it makes up almost 60 percent of the content of the average American cigarette. Almost all the rest is Burley. Because it contains little or no sugar, Burley can absorb flavorings—including rum, honey, chocolate, menthol, peach, licorice, and many others—so it is often used in cigars, as well as cigarettes.

The two are harvested and prepared for sale differently. Burley tobacco plants are cut down whole and hung in a barn to dry in natural air for three to six weeks. The leaves are not removed until after curing. By contrast, Bright tobacco is picked, or "primed," a few leaves at a time, moving up from the bottom as the leaves ripen, over a period of several weeks. Much of this strenuous, time-consuming work is done at the height of the South's humid summer, when the fuzzy leaves ooze sap. Farmworkers—especially those who don't smoke—sometimes get dizzy or nauseous from handling the huge, sticky leaves.

Once picked, the Bright leaves are cured much as they were in the mid-nineteenth century. Traditionally, the leaves are tied at the stem end onto sticks, which are hung in a tall, airtight wooden curing barn. A large tin pipe, or flue, around the floor of the barn connects with an opening to the outside; this is where a fire is maintained to heat the flue. At first, the temperature in the barn is not very high, about 90°F (32°C). Over the next six to seven days, the temperature is slowly raised in stages to 165°F (74°C); during this controlled process, the chlorophyll in the leaf breaks down and the leaf turns a bright yellow, while the starch within turns to sugar and the moisture is removed. Nowadays, most farmers of flue-cured tobacco use metal bulk barns, which typically hold more than twice as much leaf as an old-fashioned barn. The bulk barns force heat through the leaves while controlling air circulation and humidity. But the picturesque wooden structures still dot the landscape in tobacco country. Before the mechanization of some farmwork and the introduction of bulk-curing barns, it took more than four hundred hours of labor to raise, harvest, and process 1 acre (0.4 hectare) of flue-cured tobacco. Today, it still takes more than two hundred hours.

After the curing is finished, the grower separates the tobacco leaves according to stalk position, color, and quality of the leaves, a process called "grading." The leaves are bundled up in burlap; each of these bundles, known as "sheets," contains about 250 pounds (114 kilograms) of leaf. The farmer hauls them to an auction warehouse, where they are weighed, regraded by a USDA inspector, and lined up in rows on the warehouse floor.

Tobacco is sold in a curious kind of dance. The buyers, leaf dealers who are purchasing on instructions from cigarette makers, line up opposite the auc-

Farmers sell their cured tobacco at auction. Each bundle, or "sheet," is marked with a ticket indicating the minimum acceptable price per pound. Any tobacco that doesn't draw a bid of at least one cent a pound more than the minimum, or support price, goes to a farmers' co-operative so that every farmer gets a full paycheck at the auction's end.

tioneer, a row of tobacco sheets between them. Walking alongside the chanting auctioneer, the buyers turn practiced eyes to each sheet, then signal their bids silently, holding up a finger, a fist, a spread palm. A warehouseman follows, marking the ticket on each sheet with the price it has sold for.

From the auction warehouse, the tobacco is taken to a processing plant where it is reinspected and regraded. The leaves are checked for any mold or spoilage, then moistened, stemmed, redried, and tightly packed into heavy cardboard cases. This processed tobacco, called "strip," typically remains in storage to age for a year or more before it is put into cigarettes. From July into November, these plants process flue-cured tobacco around the clock. Then the Burley crop arrives, and it is processed into strip from November through May.

Before the auctioning is finished, though, tobacco farmers begin to get ready for the next season's crop–cleaning out greenhouses, clearing fields, planting winter rotation crops. With that, another thirteen-month year begins.

Jackie Thompson of Rolesville, North Carolina, raises flue-cured tobacco the modern way.[1]

In February 1998, Thompson started the year's crop in his greenhouse, as he has done since the early nineties. Over the course of two days, a machine placed seed into 3,642 plastic foam trays that would hold 288 plants each, or about 1.05 million plants. The trays sat on 4 inches (10 centimeters) of water in a "floatbed." The plants were allowed to grow about

8 inches (20 centimeters) tall, with pencil-thin stalks. As they grew in the greenhouse's shelter, the seedlings had to be clipped two or three times, so that they would be heartier, healthier, and more uniform in size for transplanting.

For a while that year, it seemed that transplanting time would never come. Relentless spring rains kept the fields too soggy. Finally, in May, the weather broke. Along with flue-cured farmers throughout North Carolina, Thompson got his crop into the field. By the beginning of July, the plants were about 5 feet (1.5 meters) tall, most with a spray of trumpet-shaped pink flowers at the top. Thompson's crew of fourteen workers walked through the fields, row by row, topping each plant and tossing the flowers on the ground, snapping off the small suckers from the axils of some leaves. Once the topping was done, the men again traveled down the rows of tobacco and sprayed the top of each plant with a sucker retardant. Because the leaves grow roughly in pairs, the chemical trickles down from leaf to leaf at the points where they join the stalk. Gazing at the lush, dark green plants, Thompson observed, "This is as pretty a crop of tobacco as I've seen in this field."

The land was not his own–Thompson farms about 100 acres (40 hectares) of tobacco, but he owns only the 2 acres (0.8 hectares) surrounding his house. He rents the land he farms from several owners, along with the tobacco quota, or government-allotted growing rights, to go with it. His field laborers are Mexican migrant workers, a number of whom have returned to his farm for several years. Most speak no

English; Thompson has had to learn enough Spanish to communicate with them. It's a different world from the one in which his father, grandfather, and great-grandfather raised tobacco.

Thompson can recall helping to take cured tobacco out of the old barn when he was about four years old. As he got older, he learned to pull the leaves off the plants, an activity at which youngsters competed to see who was the fastest primer. Later, he attended business college, planning to get off the farm. But after a few job interviews, he reconsidered. "What's going to happen if I leave?" he asked himself. "What's going to happen to Mama and Daddy?" What he really wanted, Thompson decided, was a life just like his parents'. In 1971 at age twenty, he told his father that he would follow in his footsteps and take over the family farm.

The next year the Thompsons installed metal bulk-curing barns. For a time Jackie's father continued getting up at night to check the temperature in the barns, even though it was controlled by machines. It was a hard habit to break, after so many years of having to tend the fires for his wooden curing barns around the clock.

Jackie Thompson had seen a lot of changes in the tobacco business in his forty-seven years. As he drove his truck along a bumpy dirt road one day and surveyed his ripening 1998 crop, he pointed out places where land across from the tobacco fields had been divided into small lots for houses. Newcomers buy small lots like those, he said, even though they can see there are farm fields across the road. Then they build houses, move in, and complain about the smell of the farming chemicals.

More worrisome, though, were changes that seemed to be unfolding in Washington, D.C. Congress was considering ending the price-support system for tobacco and enacting laws that could cut sales of tobacco products. Uncertainty dogged tobacco farmers that summer, and Thompson wondered if it might be time for him to find another career.

But the crop still grew.

Thompson's workers primed his tobacco and hung it in the bulk barns, starting in late July. It took three passes through the fields to harvest all the tobacco, four or so leaves per plant on each pass. On a sunny day in September, with about half of the crop harvested, a truck sat near the bulk barns behind his house, piled high with sheets of cured leaf ready to take to auction. Green and yellow scraps of leaf lay on the ground, and the air was filled with the sweet, strawlike scent of cured leaf. Next to one of the fields, workers pulled golden leaves out of two other bulk barns, piled them onto burlap sheets, and tied up the corners, while the barn motors hummed in the background.

In mid-October, Thompson watched one of the year's final auctions with satisfaction, chatting with other farmers about the new trend of bringing leaf in 750-pound (340-kilogram) bales, instead of the smaller, loosely packed sheets. Auction time is the farmers' payday, and 1998 had turned out to be a good year. The land he farmed had yielded abundance, about 3,000 pounds (1,362 kilograms) of to-

VOICE . . . FROM THE FARM

"Years ago, it was a much smaller opera-
tion. . . . The plowing was done with mules
and horses. . . . But everybody worked,
everybody worked on the farm. . . . Daddy
would go to check his barns. . . . While he
was gone, us children would get us the
prettiest leaves and roll them up and make
cigars. And we'd put them on the furnace
because that was hot and it would dry them
out, and we would smoke them. Roll that leaf
up and make us a cigar, and smoke it. . . .

"I can remember that my brothers. . . .
would get up early enough in the morning to
go and pull off the tobacco, about two
hundred sticks of tobacco, and put it in a
pile. And my mama and daddy would grade
all day long and pack it in a big compart-
ment in the strip house, and at night, after
we had supper, we went back to the strip
house, and we'd be in there many a night
until twelve o'clock tying all that tobacco.
And our studying was done by a lantern
light, and it was just a dim light. . . . We'd

study all of our lessons and then we would help tie that tobacco and we'd go home so tired and sleepy. . . .

"I can remember, back when we were married, I would go to the barn with Ellis. We had two barns. And I would let him sleep the first half of the night, and I tended those barns. . . . And I would do that till twelve o'clock, and then he would look after them till day, because the next morning we would have to go to work. That's the way we did it then. . . .

"Nobody in our family smokes, but it was their choice. And a lot of people smoke and that was their choice, nobody made them smoke. . . . I don't think that it probably does anybody good, but if they get satisfaction out of it and if that's what they want to do, why, that's what they do. But I'm still happy that none of mine smoke."

Louise Ayscue Thompson, age eighty-one, mother of Jackie Thompson, Rolesville, North Carolina, July 2, 1998 bacco an acre. The leaf dealers were buying every sheet on the floor of the New Dollar-High Price Warehouse in Henderson, North Carolina. They were paying more than the minimum prices, in some cases sixty-two cents a pound more. By the end of auction season, Thompson had gotten over his doubts.

Jackie Thompson's family has raised tobacco for at least five generations. He doesn't smoke, nor do his wife or children. But he considers that a choice he is entitled to make, just as he believes a smoker has the right to choose to smoke. "They say it's a health issue," he said. "And I'm aware that anything that anybody introduces into their body has an effect on their body—whether it be smoking, alcohol, or whatever you eat every day of your life." But in his case, he said, he has to consider the fact that tobacco income supports his family. It is also a matter of preserving a heritage.

"When I decided I wanted to be on the farm, I felt as though that's where I needed to be...because I was the youngest child," he said. "And I felt as though if I left and went away from home, that my daddy would not be able to carry on the tradition that he wanted to carry on. I wouldn't change anything in the world that I've done. . . .

"I believe in tobacco. . . . I do believe that it's an honorable profession."

Chapter Six

LEAVES OF GOLD

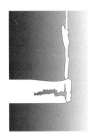 Since Europeans first came to dominate tobacco cultivation, the industry has produced big money. One tobacco historian asserts that farmers, manufacturers, and governments have grown as addicted to tobacco money as users have to its nicotine.

The economics of tobacco are complex, but a good place to start unraveling the web of money is a look at where tobacco-buying dollars go. In 1995, American consumers spent about $50 billion on tobacco products, about 95 percent of it for cigarettes. Of that, slightly less than $1 billion—or 2 cents on the dollar—went to the purchase of leaf from American tobacco farmers. Cigarette factory workers, whose wages are among the highest in any manufacturing jobs, were paid $1.3 billion. About $5 billion was spent on advertising. The federal government claims $5.9 billion a year in excise taxes, and state and local governments take in $7.7 billion in excise taxes annually. The states also collect about $2 billion a year in sales taxes on tobacco products.

The entire business–from field to supermarket shelf–generates about half a million jobs, of which the U.S. Department of Agriculture estimates 156,000 are on the farm. Cigarette manufacturers have reaped great public-relations benefits by promoting the image of the heroic family farmer who would be hard-pressed if he couldn't grow tobacco. There is some validity to this. Flue-cured tobacco sells for about $4,000 an acre–far more than the $500 yielded by cotton, the next-highest-grossing crop grown in tobacco areas. Also, unlike other crops, tobacco growing has remained relatively small-scale. The average American flue-cured tobacco farm consists of about 30 acres (12 hectares); Burley crops average only about 5 acres (2 hectares). So the "family farmer" is no mere mirage of advertising.

But a recent USDA study found that most tobacco-farming jobs are part-time, and relatively few people who work the land depend on tobacco for the bulk of their income. While many growers work at it full-time, the USDA says, most have other jobs off the farm and/or grow other crops or raise livestock as well. In fact, the amount of land planted in tobacco has been declining over the past three decades. Between 1965 and 1998, tobacco acreage shrank by 20 percent, from 942,000 acres (381,227 hectares) to 749,000 acres (303,120 hectares).

Because it brings in so much income, though, tobacco often serves as the "cash crop" that makes up for the smaller profits of other crops on a farm. Among Burley farmers, for example, tobacco takes up only about 3 percent of the average farm's acreage but accounts for more than half of the farm's income.

Part of the reason tobacco farming has remained so profitable is the price support program of the federal government. Many people mistakenly believe the government subsidizes, or makes direct payments to, tobacco farmers. Actually, the program that originated in the Great Depression keeps prices up by limiting the amount of leaf that farmers bring to market. In theory, when less leaf is available, buyers will be willing to pay more for each pound. In practice, it doesn't always work this way—so before each growing season, the USDA sets minimum prices that farmers can count on for each grade of leaf.

At the auction house, if no buyer bids higher than the government-set price for a particular sheet of leaf, the sheet goes to an organization called the Tobacco Cooperative Stabilization Corporation, which pays the grower the guaranteed minimum price. The money with which the cooperatives pay for unsold tobacco comes from federal government loans, which must be repaid with interest. The cooperatives process and store the leaf, then sell it later when they can get a better price. By law, the price-support program must be run at no net cost to American taxpayers, except for the $14 million a year the USDA spends administering it.

The right to grow a certain amount of tobacco is called a "quota." The USDA adjusts the amount of quota that farmers get each year, depending on how much leaf it expects buyers to want. This information, in turn, comes primarily from the cigarette makers. The total tobacco quota for 1998, for instance, was about 1.5 billion pounds (681 million kilograms).

The 1930s law that established the quota system tied the growing rights to the land. That is why tobacco is still farmed in the same places it was then. Current law allows quota owners to sell or rent out their growing rights, but the crop generally must be grown in the same county to which the quota is assigned. In fact, most quota owners today do not farm tobacco but rent their land and quota to growers such as Jackie Thompson. According to the USDA, there were more than 300,000 quotas in 1998, but only about 120,000 tobacco farms. Some quota owners are retired farmers who depend on that rental income. Others are far removed from the farm, including lawyers, doctors, military officers, politicians, and residents of non-tobacco states and foreign countries.

Looking at the giant tobacco industry in America, it is easy to assume that farmers and cigarette company executives are enthusiastic teammates. But because growers want to get as much money as possible for their crop while cigarette makers want to get as much leaf as possible for their money, the two are somewhat at odds. As seen in Chapter 2, this conflict between those who grow tobacco and those who market it has its roots in colonial times. In the days of Buck Duke's tobacco trust, the cigarette makers wielded complete control over what farmers earned because there was no one else the growers could sell their crop to. That enormous imbalance of power is what led to the creation of the support program, and the imbalance persists today.

For six decades after its inception in the 1930s, the price-support program was defended in Congress by lawmakers from the tobacco-growing states of the Southeast. In 1982 some members of Congress tried to kill the program; instead, a law was passed preserving the program but requiring that it be paid for by growers and buyers instead of by taxpayers. Lawmakers from many states have protected the tobacco industry in other ways as well, repeatedly exempting it from federal regulation. It is probably no coincidence that the tobacco industry contributed almost $30 million to political campaigns from 1987 to 1997. A small number of legislators refuse tobacco industry donations.

In the early 1960s, Philip Morris hit on the idea of gaining allies by making big donations to health institutions, starting with a gift of $25,000 to the Sloan-Kettering Institute, a major cancer-fighting center. Other cigarette makers soon followed suit. This was the start of a long program of buying support among social institutions. Over the decades that followed, with Philip Morris leading the way, cigarette companies gave tens of millions of dollars to organizations that would be hard-pressed to raise the money any other way. Philip Morris also has given tens of millions of dollars to social causes including civil rights, help for the homeless, and job training for disadvantaged youths, as well as to libraries and literacy-promoting organizations. The company has made large donations to African-American groups, such as the National Association for the Advancement of Colored People, the Urban League, and the United Ne-

The relationship between Congress and the tobacco growers was the subject of public outcry for decades. This scene, from 1969, shows members of a group called Legislative Action on Smoking and Health carrying a replica of a coffin as they picket outside the Capitol in support of strong anticigarette legislation.

gro College Fund. Between 1986 and 1997, it gave more than $11 million to groups fighting AIDS.

Philip Morris has also given heavily to dance companies, including Ballet Hispanico, the Alvin Ailey American Dance Theater, the Joffrey Ballet, and the American Ballet Theatre. It has supported small local theater groups and sponsored art exhibits featuring the work of women, Native Americans, African Americans, and Hispanics. In 1990 the company spent $30 million to $50 million backing a nationwide bicentennial tribute to the Bill of Rights. None of these events, of course, were meant to make people dash right out and buy Philip Morris cigarettes. Instead, the donations and sponsorships showed Americans what a patriotic and generous corporation PM was. If some of the people who benefited from the gifts spoke out in defense of the tobacco company—and some did—so much the better.

Tobacco money built the cities of Durham, North Carolina, and Richmond, Virginia. The nation's second-oldest university, the College of William and Mary, was financed with a tobacco tax, and tobacco money has been crucial to other educational institutions, such as Duke University and Wake Forest University.

The American government, too, has long been a beneficiary of vigorous tobacco sales, as have governments throughout the commercial history of tobacco. In some nations, the government itself owns the tobacco industry, a practice that dates from the early seventeenth century. The other way governments, including that of the United States, get revenue from tobacco is through taxes. As early as 1660, England depended on tobacco import taxes, or duties, for about 5 percent of total government income. Recent figures paint a more striking picture: In 1983 tobacco taxes made up 23 percent of central government revenue in Argentina and 41 percent in Haiti. Tobacco taxes account for a much smaller share of government income in the United States, but the numbers are still significant. And because tax rates have risen, tax revenue has gone up even as cigarette sales have fallen.

On the other hand, tobacco-related illnesses are costly to Americans. Calculating this cost is tricky. Researchers who have tried have come up with vastly different results. The American Cancer Society, for instance, estimates that each pack of cigarettes sold costs Americans $3.90 for medical care, lost work, and so on. Duke University economist W. Keith Viscusi, though, wrote in 1994 that smokers actually save Americans money because they die younger and therefore cost taxpayers less in Social Security payments and long-term medical expenses.

Tobacco also has created bizarre contradictions in government activities. State researchers advise tobacco farmers and work to develop new and better strains of tobacco. U.S. trade officials help American tobacco companies sell more products overseas. Meanwhile, government health agencies have worked for decades to encourage Americans to stop smoking. But the more tobacco people consume, the more money the government can make by taxing it.

As Napoléon III of France said of smoking in the mid-nineteenth century: "This vice brings in one hundred million francs in taxes every year. I will certainly forbid it at once—as soon as you can name a virtue that brings in as much revenue."[1]

CHAPTER SEVEN
REPLACEMENTS

 Cigarette companies are losing cus-
tomers in the United States. Every day,
more than 3,000 Americans quit smoking. And every day, on average, more
than 1,100 people in the United States
die from smoking. How can an industry hope to maintain its business in the
face of this shrinking consumer base?

Another set of statistics holds part of the answer.
First, more than 80 percent of adult smokers started
smoking before they were eighteen years old. Second, every day about six thousand youngsters under
eighteen light up for the first time, and about half as
many become daily smokers. You don't have to be a
mathematician to see what cigarette executives have
long known: They have to recruit "replacement"
smokers among the young.

Documents that were made public in the late
1990s show the industry's thinking. A 1975 memo
from the files of R. J. Reynolds Tobacco, for example,
asserts: "To ensure increased and longer-term growth
for Camel Filter, the brand must increase its share

penetration among the 14 to 24 age group which have a new set of more liberal values and which represent tomorrow's cigarette business."[1] The next year, an RJR planning forecast said: "The 14- to 18-year-old group is an increasing segment of the smoking population. RJR-T must soon establish a successful new brand in this market if our position in the industry is to be maintained over the long term."[2] Around the same time, Brown & Williamson marketing researchers worked on a plan to make the Viceroy brand more appealing to youngsters. Those consultants advised B&W to exploit young people's desire to rebel: "For them, a cigarette, and the whole smoking process, is part of the illicit pleasure category. . . . To the best of your ability... relate the cigarette to 'pot,' wine, beer, sex, etc."[3]

Most tobacco executives have maintained that they never set out to sell cigarettes to children or teenagers. Cigarette advertisements speak for themselves. In the 1960s, TV ads that aired with popular family shows featured characters from the shows, making it hard for children to tell the difference between entertainment and advertising. In one ad with *The Flintstones*, the cartoon characters Fred and Barney sneaked behind the house for a smoke. Barney pulled out a pack of Winstons and offered one to his friend. They praised the cigarette's flavor, and Fred added, "Yeah, Barney, Winston tastes good like a cigarette should." An ad that aired during *The Beverly Hillbillies*, another favorite with young viewers, showed mountain man Jed and all his kin driving past a Winston truck. A deep voice sang a reworked version of

Dwane Powell takes the targeting of teens by the tobacco industry to task in this cartoon from the Raleigh, North Carolina, newspaper, The News & Observer. *He portrays the link between government restrictions on the industry and the cigarette makers' efforts to compensate by recruiting a young new generation of smokers.*

the show's catchy theme song, with new lyrics hailing Winston cigarettes.[4]

Did print and television ads show cigarettes in the hands of timid, sickly, or ugly people? Never. Celebrities smoked. Mountain climbers and helicopter pilots smoked. Tanned, muscular men and shapely women smoked while romping poolside or camping out or driving fast cars. Cigarette ads portrayed a world where smokers were healthy, active, and happy, old enough to be in charge and young enough to be beautiful.

By far the most popular brand among young smokers is Marlboro, a cigarette that in the first half of the twentieth century had been promoted as a women's brand. Philip Morris executives decided to transform Marlboro's image in the 1950s. Early advertising for the new, masculine Marlboro showed virile men in a number of environments, but the character most popular with consumers was a cowboy. In the mid-sixties, the rousing music from the movie *The Magnificent Seven* became the Marlboro theme. Thirty-five years later, the Marlboro Man remained a fixture in print and billboard advertising–so familiar that some billboards showed only his eyes and the brim of his cowboy hat–and Marlboro was the biggest-selling brand in the world. Among American smokers ages twelve to eighteen, about 60 percent smoked Marlboro in 1993. The Marlboro Man, a somber-faced loner, had a different appeal than the lively, sociable young adults in the ads of other brands. He was independent, on his own, in control of a thundering herd of powerful animals, a man who could meet any challenge. As one expert on teen behavior testified in a 1998 lawsuit against Big Tobacco: "There are no parents in Marlboro Country."[5]

One of the most notorious marketing campaigns was RJR's series of ads featuring a cartoon character with a pendulous nose and the life of a party animal. Old Joe Camel was introduced in 1988, at a time

The Marlboro Man looks as cool as ever, undisturbed by the hoopla at the base of his downtown Denver billboard. The scene is taking place on June 20, 1997, the day tobacco companies and state attorneys general announced an agreement requiring the companies to pay billions of dollars to the states to compensate for money the states had spent taking care of sick smokers.

when Philip Morris's Marlboro cowboy had galloped away with the youth market. Ad designers decked out Joe Camel in tuxedo and sunglasses and surrounded him with gorgeous human women. Joe Camel showed up on clothing, mugs, sandals, and merchandise coupons. Collector packs were illustrated with pictures of Old Joe on the beach, riding a motorcycle, or playing a saxophone.

Antismoking activists reacted with outrage, saying the campaign was an obvious attempt to appeal to children. Studies showed that the cartoon was indeed making an impression. In late 1991 the *Journal of the American Medical Association* reported that almost a third of three-year-olds recognized the cartoon camel and knew it had something to do with cigarettes, and 90 percent of six-year-olds understood this. Among high-school students, 98 percent understood Joe's connection with the Camel brand. Before 1988, Camel cigarettes had had the image of "a harsh, old product,"[6] according to the RJR executive behind the Joe Camel campaign. Fewer than 1 percent of underage smokers used the brand. By the mid-nineties, almost a third were Camel smokers. In 1997, under pressure from antismoking activists and government regulators, RJR dropped the cartoon character from its advertising.

Philip Morris took a more subtle tack by attaching the names of its cigarette brands to sporting events and concerts. After TV ads were banned in 1971, the company put up billboards in baseball stadiums, getting the Marlboro logo beamed into living rooms where people watched games on television. Philip Morris also took the lead in getting its brands shown in movies, a practice known as "product placement." It's no accident that Lois Lane smokes Marlboros in the 1980 *Superman II*, or that Lark cigarettes show up in the James Bond movie *Licence to Kill.* The cigarette makers paid tens of thousands of dollars for those appearances.

Among the tobacco industry documents uncovered by lawsuits is a 1979 letter from the maker of *Superman II* to Philip Morris outlining the product placement agreement, including a promise that the Marlboro brand name would appear "in a major scene in the Film involving 'Ursa,' . . . 'General Zod' ... and 'Superman.'" In return, PM was to pay 20,000 pounds sterling, or about $42,000. A 1983 letter from actor Sylvester Stallone "guarantee[s] that [he] will use Brown & Williamson tobacco products in no less than five feature films" and notes "that Brown & Williamson will pay a fee of $500,000.00." An internal B&W memo from the same year frets over the fact that throughout the movie *Apocalypse Now*, actor Martin Sheen smokes Marlboros. But, the writer seems to gloat, the exposure was probably only worth half of the $200,000 that Philip Morris is said to have paid for the product placement.[7]

Another kind of placement put tobacco products right in front of even small children: displays in grocery stores and supermarkets. Cigarette packs were sold from shelves at a child's eye level, just like chocolate bars and bubble gum. Pouches and cans of smokeless tobacco are nearly indistinguishable from candy packages, featuring cheerful pictures of dogs or Indians and words such as "wintergreen" and "cherry," as well as a brand name associated with sugary chewing gum, Beech-Nut.

Cigarette companies gave and sold promotional items such as T-shirts, backpacks, hats, and gym bags to young people. This, too, appeared to influence youths to start smoking. In 1993 researchers in California began a study of teenagers who had never smoked and had no intention of doing so. Some of them owned promotional items that bore the logos of cigarette brands. Three years later, the researchers found, those who owned the promotional items were three times as likely to have started smoking as those who did not own any. Another study looked at magazines that had a lot of readers in the twelve-to-seventeen age range, tallying the ads for cigarette brands that were most popular with youngsters (Marlboro, Newport, Camel, Kool, and Winston). In magazines for which one third of the readers fell into this age group, advertising for the "youth brands" was five times as heavy as that for brands that were smoked mostly by adults. Furthermore, 86 percent of underage smokers preferred the three most heavily advertised brands—Marlboro, Camel, and Newport.

For almost twenty years, from the late 1970s to the early 1990s, smoking among high-school students steadily decreased. In 1992, however, the trend turned around. According to researchers at the University of Michigan, about 29 percent of high-school seniors smoked daily in 1976; that figure dropped to 17 percent by 1992. Four years later, however, ev-

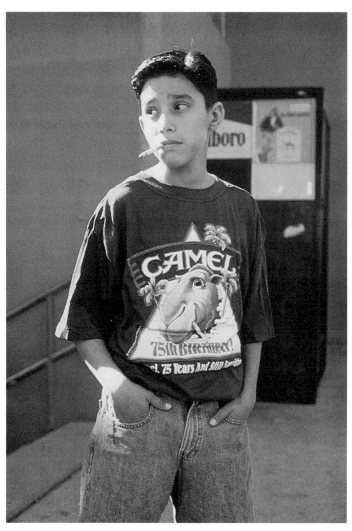

A portrait of targeting: a boy, too young to smoke, proudly sports his Joe Camel T-shirt. Behind him is the vending machine, covered with smoking ads, from which he probably purchased the cigarette hanging from his mouth.

eryday smoking among seniors had risen again to 22 percent. When the researchers in 1997 looked at how many high-school students had smoked at least once in the past month, they found a similar rise: About 36.4 percent had smoked in the past month in 1997, compared to only about 27.5 percent in 1991.

Most alarming was the sudden rise in smoking among African-American youths, especially girls. Smoking among black teenagers had declined dramatically since 1976. Then, between 1991 and 1997, the rate almost doubled among black teenage males (from 14.2 percent to 28.2 percent) and increased by about half (from 11.3 percent to 17.4 percent) among females. Health officials had interviewed young smokers in the past and had found that many black girls saw smoking as low class and so were less likely to smoke than white girls, who thought smoking was glamorous. Overall, smoking among black teens increased three times as fast as among white teens in those six years. No one could explain the turnaround.

Other ominous developments showed up in 1998 government reports. In August the U.S. Department of Health and Human Services said that while the smoking rate remained about the same for youths fourteen and older, the rate among twelve- and thirteen-year-olds jumped significantly in a single year, from 7.3 percent in 1996 to 9.7 percent in 1997. The Centers for Disease Control and Prevention (CDC) reported in October that youth smoking had climbed significantly since 1988, the year the cartoon Joe Camel debuted: The number of twelve- to seventeen-year-olds taking their first puff had risen 30 percent,

VOICE...OF YOUTH

"It's appalling-slash-surprising that an industry that is so blatantly false—everything about it is false, from their research to their marketing to their congressional testimony—has been allowed to stay in business, and not only stay in business but to be profitable for so many years. I think that needs to change. I think everybody's to blame for it: The industry itself, of course. Congress and the lawmakers we've had for years, for not taking a stand against them. And the people for letting it happen.... Politicians are more than happy to talk but are reluctant to take action. That's where grassroots efforts come in. That's where people have to step up."

Jared Perez, age eighteen, of Belleair Beach, Florida, teen marketing director for Truth, Florida Pilot Program on Tobacco Control, October 28, 1998

and the number who began smoking daily had jumped 50 percent. As a result, the CDC said, about 1.5 million more youths were daily smokers than would have been if smoking rates had remained at the pre-1988 levels.

By the end of 1998, the picture brightened a bit: The University of Michigan researchers found that teenagers' smoking had leveled off and even declined slightly in some groups.

Many youths who use cigarettes plan to smoke for a while and to quit when they get older. Time, however, is not on their side. The longer a person smokes, the stronger his or her nicotine addiction becomes. A 1997 study found that almost three quarters of high-school students who had ever been daily smokers had tried to quit. Only about one in eight succeeded.

In Florida, a group of teenagers set out to rescue their generation from Big Tobacco by launching their own marketing campaign. In April 1998 the two-year effort began, supported by $50 million the state had won in a lawsuit against the tobacco industry (see Chapter 10). The premise was something that comes as naturally as breathing to a teenager: rebellion. This time, though, the teens in the campaign urged their peers to rebel against the well-paid men in business suits who were trying to get youths addicted for life. One high-school junior involved in the campaign explained to a *Los Angeles Times* reporter: "Smoking is not rebellious or individualistic. Smokers are manipulated into doing exactly what tobacco companies want."[8] The state hired a Miami ad agency to work under the direction of about a dozen Florida teenagers in creating guerrilla-style messages.

The teens came up with a brand name for themselves, Truth, and a slogan: "Their brand is lies. Our brand is truth." They put up a World Wide Web page

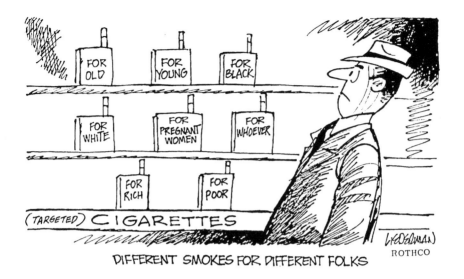

FOR OLD · FOR YOUNG · FOR BLACK · FOR WHITE · FOR PREGNANT WOMEN · FOR WHOEVER · FOR RICH · FOR POOR

(TARGETED) CIGARETTES

LIEDERMAN)
ROTHCO

DIFFERENT SMOKES FOR DIFFERENT FOLKS

Syndicated cartoonist Liederman laughs at the cigarette industry's practice of targeting—but until the government finally cracked down, especially on the targeting of children, it was a highly successful strategy.

(www.wholetruth.com), blitzed radio and TV airwaves, and placed full-page ads in major newspapers. One ad, which ran in *The Washington Post* and other big papers, showed a girl wearing a black ski mask. The ransom note she held read: "We may be hostages. But today, we're the ones making the demands. We're truth. A generation that's tired of being lied to about tobacco. Tired of replacing the 1,000 customers tobacco kills every day. Tired of being a target." They hired a plane to fly over race fans at the Marlboro Grand Prix, towing a banner that read: "By the end of this race, 3,000 kids will have started smoking."[9]

That auto race was one of a variety of events that tobacco companies have supported financially, at a cost of tens of millions of dollars. In return, the companies gain a positive image in the eyes of fans. Philip Morris courted the favor of young women with its Virginia Slims tennis tournament and of young men with the Marlboro Grand Prix. R. J. Reynolds's parent company, RJR Nabisco, countered by sponsoring a women's golf tournament called the Dinah Shore Open and the NASCAR Winston Cup Racing Series.

Cigarette makers also made a point of pursuing nonwhite customers, with marketing plans that involved "ethnic factors," according to documents released by Liggett in 1997. One report said: "Spanish and Negro groups like to purchase only the best of everything–they are not looking for bargains." To entice Hispanic and black smokers, "there must be a racial slant in the marketing efforts," the report continued, noting also that "promotion must be smart and sophisticated" to appeal to the Jewish market.[10]

But even though Big Tobacco devoted so much attention to enhancing its image and targeting ads at specific groups, the overall smoking rate in the United States continued dropping. So in the 1980s, the biggest cigarette makers boosted their efforts to look to other countries. What they found were more profits than they had ever made.

CHAPTER EIGHT

THINKING GLOBALLY

A century ago, Buck Duke recognized that he did not have to limit his tobacco empire to his own country. But even he would probably have been astonished at how far American tobacco companies have reached into other countries. For the industry leaders, Philip Morris and RJR, international sales quadrupled from 1986 to 1996. By 1998, the two companies drew more than half their sales from foreign smokers. Today, it is hard to travel anywhere and not be greeted by the Marlboro Man.

American and British cigarette companies made inroads in Europe several decades ago, then moved into Latin America and Africa. But Big Tobacco's campaign to win customers abroad made its greatest strides in the 1980s, while per capita cigarette use in the United States was falling and pressure from anti-smoking advocates was on the rise. It happened that the United States faced a record trade deficit in the mid-eighties, meaning that it was spending much more importing goods from other nations than it was earning by selling American goods overseas. The federal government was eager to find a way to restore balance between the nation's imports and exports. That desire meshed neatly with the wishes of the cigarette companies.

The push began in Asia, where enormous markets awaited. In Japan, South Korea, Taiwan, and Thailand, cigarettes were made and sold by state-run tobacco monopolies that generated large amounts of revenue for the governments. Those countries were experiencing rapid economic growth in the mid-eighties, and their citizens wanted to spend their new wealth on high-quality and prestigious products. The American cigarette was one of those goods. But the nations had tight restrictions on imported cigarettes. Japan, for example, kept American cigarettes out with high tariffs, or import taxes. In South Korea, it was a crime to buy or sell even a pack of foreign cigarettes.

The United States imported a wide variety of goods from those four Asian nations and had run up a large trade imbalance with them. Alarmed, the U.S. Congress considered taking action to make goods from these countries more expensive in the United States so that Americans would buy fewer foreign-made products—unless those countries allowed the sale of more American-made goods in their territory. With the support of President Ronald Reagan, a government agency called the Office of the U.S. Trade Representative (USTR) launched an investigation into unfair trading practices by the Asian nations. Under the 1974 Trade Act, the investigation could have led to retaliation by the United States.

The threat proved effective. In 1986, Japan agreed to let American cigarettes in, along with the advertising and promotions that would inevitably come with them. Taiwan and South Korea followed.

Philip Morris swept into Japan with its Virginia Slims brand, targeting women, few of whom smoked before American cigarettes arrived. Before long, RJR brought in Joe Camel. The Japanese tobacco monopoly fought the competition with its own brands aimed at women and young people, and within a year cigarettes were the second most heavily advertised product on television in Tokyo. In Taiwan, RJR sponsored a dance at a disco popular with teenagers in the capital, Taipei. Anyone who showed up with five empty Winston packs was admitted free. Billboards for foreign cigarettes sprang up within sight of high schools. South Korea, which had only recently banned all cigarette advertising, consented to magazine ads, shop signs, and cigarette company sponsorship of sporting and cultural events. Almost immediately, American tobacco companies pumped $25 million into advertising there.

Sales in those three countries reflected the new, sophisticated American marketing techniques. A year after entering South Korea, American brands accounted for 6 percent of cigarette sales. Foreign brands held more than 20 percent of the market in

Taiwan within two years, and Taiwanese health officials noted a steady rise in smoking by high-school students. In Japan a decade later, imported cigarettes commanded more than 20 percent of sales, and smoking by women was higher than it had ever been, especially among young women entering college.

Among the four Asian nations that Big Tobacco tried to penetrate in the 1980s, only Thailand successfully resisted. The USTR, supported by the new administration of President George Bush, pushed in 1989 for removal of Thailand's trade barriers to a number of American products. But public-health officials in Thailand banded together with the nation's tobacco monopoly to oppose letting American cigarettes in. The dispute ended up before an international trade panel, which ruled that Thailand had to allow the import of tobacco products, but it could ban advertising as long as the ban was also applied to Thai products. With help from American antismoking activists, Thailand enacted some of the world's strictest tobacco control laws.

The Thais' resistance sparked an antismoking movement in Asia that agitated for warning labels, restrictions on sales, and other measures. By the mid-nineties, more than thirty Asian nations had enacted tobacco control laws. The movement also heightened public interest in curbing tobacco use. Many younger Japanese women expecting their first child quit smoking during their pregnancy. Japanese husbands found themselves banished outdoors when they smoked at home—a practice so common that the men were nicknamed *hotaru-zoku*, or "firefly of the family," because when they smoked outside in the dark the glowing ends of their cigarettes looked like fireflies.

The collapse of Communist governments in Eastern Europe at the end of the 1980s provided another opportunity for Big Tobacco to move into markets from which it had been shut out. There, it did more than just import cigarettes made by well-paid American workers. National economies were in ruins after decades of domination by the Soviet Union: Factories were crumbling, pay was low, consumer goods were of wretched quality. American and European tobacco companies came to the rescue, bringing outdated factories back to vitality, generating jobs, and making milder-tasting American-style cigarettes available.

Within five years, the foreign companies bought control of all the cigarette factories in the Czech Republic and Slovakia, all the state-owned cigarette factories in Hungary, and almost half of the cigarette-making capacity of the former Soviet Union. The companies' products found eager customers. American cigarettes are prized in Eastern Europe and are sometimes even used in place of money. Struggling governments gained new infusions of money from cigarette taxes, and the companies sponsored sports and cultural events as they had for decades in the United States.

The biggest prize of all—if American tobacco companies could win it—would be China. In that nation, the most populous in the world, there are more than 300 million smokers, most of them male, who consume one third of the world's cigarettes. And it is

While other Western industries hesitated to invest in the former Soviet bloc, fearing they would lose money in the politically unstable nations, Philip Morris, R. J. Reynolds, and other tobacco giants swiftly moved in.

one of the few countries where per capita cigarette use is rising. Although China restricts imports, American companies promoted their products with an eye toward the future. Philip Morris put the Marlboro name on billboards and murals in Chinese cities. Athletes could play Marlboro League soccer, and radio fans could listen to the *Marlboro Music Hour.* In keeping with Chinese cultural sensibilities, any Marlboro Country picture that showed a horse

VOICES . . . AT ODDS

"What many countries have now is a window of opportunity . . . to adopt legislation, for example, banning cigarette advertising, restricting smoking in public places, cracking down on the sale of tobacco products to kids . . . all the kind of things which they probably couldn't do five or ten years from now. I think the window will close as quickly as the tobacco sales abroad expand."

John F. Banzhaf III, founder of Action on Smoking and Health, October 27, 1998

"We sold a record 711.5 billion cigarettes outside the United States last year. . . . The growth of our brands was led by a gain of more than 5 percent for Marlboro, the best-selling cigarette in the world. . . . In Poland, we recorded exceptional volume growth, led by Marlboro. . . . Our share in Japan topped 17 percent for the first time, boosted by the rapid growth of Marlboro, which became the number one international brand in the country."

Philip Morris Companies Inc. 1997 Annual Report

showed a white one because the Chinese consider it a symbol of good luck. Salem, an RJR brand, became popular with young women. Its logo showed up on cafe clocks, menu holders, and ashtrays. There was a Salem tennis tournament, as well as a Kent (a Lorillard brand) billiards contest. To young adults in China, American cigarettes are a sign of status and achievement.

American cigarette companies weren't allowed to storm into China, which unlike the nations of Eastern Europe still has a Communist government. But they managed to edge in. Philip Morris and RJR partnered with the government tobacco company in producing cigarettes. In Vietnam, another Communist Asian nation, Philip Morris and British-American Tobacco forged similar partnerships, and RJR opened its own Camel factory.

The globalization of Big Tobacco has also reached clear back to the industry's roots—literally. With the help and encouragement of American tobacco companies, farmers in other countries have learned how to grow tobacco that rivals American-grown leaf in taste and quality. And because their costs are much lower, they can grow it more cheaply. Brazil, Zimbabwe, Malawi, Turkey, and a few other countries have become major exporters of cigarette tobacco in the past two decades. In the middle of the twentieth century, the United States accounted for about 60 percent of the world's tobacco exports; by the end of the century, that figure had dropped to about 10 percent. In 1998, Malawi was the world's second-biggest producer of Burley tobacco, behind the United States; Brazil and Zimbabwe ranked right behind the United States as the world's biggest exporters of flue-cured tobacco.

The advances by farmers in other countries, particularly in Brazil, were no accident of history. Leaf dealers working for American tobacco companies put Brazilian farmers under contract and work closely with them. The companies provide the farmers with seed, fertilizer, and pesticides, and give the farmers financial help to buy land or build curing barns. Processing plants the leaf dealers have installed in Brazil are as clean and modern as any in the United States, but the farming is still done the ancient way, by dirt-poor farmers who use oxen to pull their plows. During growing season, American agronomists visit farms and give advice. Between seasons, the tobacco companies offer seminars to teach the growers new farming techniques. The result: cured tobacco that compares in quality to that grown in the United States but sells for about one third the price. Not surprisingly, U.S. tobacco farmers have been pinched by this competition.

As the tobacco industry has become international, the antismoking movement has followed it. Smokers in a number of nations have sued cigarette companies. Health activists are taking on tobacco in Europe and Asia with programs modeled after those developed in the United States. They have learned to reach across national borders to share strategies on how to keep children away from tobacco and how to persuade lawmakers to enact tobacco control statutes. Under pressure from these advocates, governments in Asia and Eastern Europe have banned or restricted cigarette advertising. Hong Kong, Singapore, and Thailand require strongly worded warning labels on cigarettes. Australia requires a warning label over at least a quarter of the surface of cigarette packs, and Canada requires one that covers a third. Tobacco opponents in other countries have been able to get government action more quickly than their American counterparts because the tobacco industry doesn't have the political power elsewhere that it has in the United States.

Big Tobacco expanded its reach in another significant way in the past few decades: It became a major force in the food industry. Philip Morris and RJR launched the drive in the mid-eighties. At that time, the antismoking movement was clearly gaining power, and the companies wanted to use their huge cigarette profits to get into businesses that were not so vulnerable to attack. RJR bought Canada Dry, Sunkist, and giant Nabisco, whose products include Oreo cookies, Ritz crackers, and Planters peanuts; the combined company was renamed RJR Nabisco. Philip Morris bought the food conglomerate General Foods and the dairy products maker Kraft Inc., eventually combining them as Kraft Foods Inc.; its brands include Jell-O, Grape-Nuts, Maxwell House, and Oscar Mayer.

The diversification didn't end at food. Philip Morris also owns Miller Brewing Co., along with financial services companies; until 1997, it also owned the real estate company that developed the city of Mission Viejo, California. Lorillard Tobacco Company was bought by the hotel and insurance conglomerate Loews Corporation in the 1960s. Liggett Group is part of a real estate and finance company called Brooke Group. And Brown & Williamson Tobacco Corporation's parent BAT Industries is also in the insurance and financial service businesses.

With its array of non-tobacco businesses and its growing presence overseas, Big Tobacco gradually put together a global enterprise that could survive and prosper even without the help of smokers in the United States.

Judith Mackay, a Hong Kong physician who has campaigned for tobacco control laws across Asia, noted in 1996 that despite some successes her task remained daunting. "People in America assume that because cigarette use is coming down there, somehow the war against tobacco is being won. But it's not. It's just being shifted from the rich countries to the poorer ones. At best we're waging guerrilla warfare against a powerful army, and on a global basis I fear that we're still losing."[1]

CHAPTER NINE

UNDER FIRE

 Cigarettes, when used as the manufac-
turers intend them to be used, make
the user sick–sometimes fatally so.
This much has long been established.
What remains to be answered as the
twentieth century draws to a close is
the question of responsibility: Whose
fault is it, and who should pay the medical bills?

Since the 1950s, when the first major studies
linked smoking to deadly illnesses, smokers have tried
to take Big Tobacco to court to make the industry
pay for the diseases caused by its products. Time and
again, cigarette makers fended off those claims by
contending that they did not force anyone to smoke–
that smokers made that choice for themselves and
therefore should bear full responsibility for the consequences.

The first of these suits was filed in 1954 by the
widow of a man who had died of lung cancer; the
case dragged on for thirteen years, and then was
dropped. In the four decades that followed that case,
Big Tobacco did not pass a day without a lawsuit pend-

ing or threatened against it. Smokers or their survivors filed more than eight hundred suits. Twenty-three actually went to trial, and the tobacco industry lost only one. That verdict was overturned on appeal. Although it spent millions of dollars fighting lawsuits, for forty years Big Tobacco maintained a perfect record of never paying a cent in damages.

Civil lawsuits against the tobacco industry have been based on a concept called product liability. When a company sells its products, it is implying to the buyers that the products are safe to use. (The law recognizes that some products, such as sharp knives or blowtorches, are hazardous by their nature but are also useful and so are not "unreasonably dangerous.") Lawsuits against Big Tobacco have come in three "waves." The initial wave lasted from 1954 to 1973, after the threat of lung cancer first made front-page news. These suits were brought by individual people, who had no hope of matching the kind of financial and legal might that Big Tobacco had on its side. The industry could always persist in court until its opponents ran out of money, became too exhausted to fight, or died.

The so-called second wave swelled with the 1980s movement for consumers' rights and the growing public concern with toxic substances. This wave lasted from 1983 to 1992, and within it were the beginnings of serious damage to Big Tobacco's rock-solid position.

In 1983 a New Jersey woman named Rose Cipollone sued Liggett Group, Philip Morris, and Loews, the conglomerate that had bought Lorillard.

Her suit claimed that the companies had failed to warn her that their cigarettes could make her sick. Cipollone had smoked about a pack and a half of cigarettes a day for forty-one years–most of those years before warning labels were put on packs. When she filed her suit against the makers of the brands she had smoked, she was already dying of cancer at age fifty-seven. Cipollone said she had started smoking in imitation of the glamorous movie stars she idolized when she was a teenager. By the time the government required warning labels on cigarette packages in the 1960s, she had no desire to quit.

Big Tobacco founded its defense on two oddly mismatched assertions: In the first place, the industry maintained, no one had proved that cigarettes cause cancer and, in the second place, the statistical link between smoking and disease had been so widely publicized that Rose Cipollone had known the risk she was taking and had chosen to take it anyway. Cipollone's lawyer set out to show that at the same time tobacco executives publicly denied the danger, they knew perfectly well about tobacco's health hazards and conspired to hide that information. Rose Cipollone's suit didn't come to trial until 1988, more than three years after she died. In the end, the jury awarded her husband $400,000–the first time a jury had awarded damages in a tobacco suit. The tobacco companies appealed, and the award was overturned. Big Tobacco had once again gotten out of a suit without paying a plaintiff. But it had cost the companies about $50 million in legal expenses to do so.

Once the question of the liability of the tobacco manufacturers was opened, the full extent of the health risks associated with smoking were publicized. Cartoonist Powell looks at the plight of the smoker in relation to the heretofore cavalier attitude of the tobacco industry executives.

Most significant in the long term, the Cipollones' lawyer managed, for the first time, to force thousands of documents out of industry files. In more than thirty years of litigation, no one outside the industry had seen what really went on behind the smoke curtain.

Many of those documents contradicted Big Tobacco's public insistence that nicotine was not an addictive drug. Typical was a 1972 memo from a Philip Morris psychologist that said: "The physiological effect serves as the primary incentive [to smoke]; all other incentives are secondary. . . . The cigarette should be conceived not as a product, but as a package. The product is nicotine. . . . Think of the cigarette pack as a storage container for a day's supply of nicotine. Think of the cigarette as a dispenser for a dose unit of nicotine."[1]

Other papers released in the case showed that the industry had, in fact, believed in the 1960s that cigarettes were dangerous, and companies had hired scientists to work on solutions. One former Liggett researcher who testified at the trial had discovered that adding a heavy metal called palladium to cigarettes substantially decreased the number of cancers they caused. But, after almost twenty years of research and millions of dollars spent, the palladium project had been killed by the company. If Liggett tried to market a "safer" cigarette, company lawyers reasoned, that would amount to a claim that the cigarettes had a health benefit, which would open the way for the Food and Drug Administration to try to regulate cigarettes. Furthermore, it would be the same as admitting the company's other cigarettes were not safe. And that, in turn, would lead to a torrent of product liability suits.

These were the twin nightmares of Big Tobacco: regulation and lawsuits. Fear of the latter was the reason the industry was willing to pour millions of dollars into every court case. The companies believed that any loss in court, even any out of court settlement, could ultimately lead to their being sued out of business. Company lawyers realized that if outsiders became aware of the research going on inside Big Tobacco's own labs, the information would give powerful ammunition to the industry's enemies. Although the companies competed with each other in the marketplace, their attorneys worked together to defend the industry as a whole. Some of the counselors ordered that all scientific information should be under the control of the companies' legal departments. That way, if a plaintiff's lawyer tried to get the documents for a lawsuit, the companies could claim attorney-client privilege. This legal doctrine allows attorneys and their clients to keep private their communications in preparing a legal case. Frustrated tobacco scientists, meanwhile, pressed their companies to be more truthful with the public and make an open effort to manufacture cigarettes that could give smokers the nicotine they wanted without delivering a load of cancer-causing agents in the process.

The scientists lost. By 1975 researchers at five of the major cigarette companies had figured out ways to make "safer" cigarettes. But it was too late to market these. Their appearance would invite lawsuits. Furthermore, the lab reports and other paperwork generated by these efforts could be devastating in court. So the companies started shutting down their labs. Between 1970 and 1984, R. J. Reynolds, the British tobacco industry, and Philip Morris dismantled labs and reassigned or fired scientists.

It turned out that the lawyers had been right about the threat to the industry from its own internal papers. In the third wave of suits, the dam burst: The small stream of information that started getting out in the Cipollone case gave way in the 1990s to a deluge of documents that would profoundly and permanently reshape the landscape.

The flood arose partly from the impulsive actions of a $9-an-hour legal clerk in Louisville, Kentucky, around the same time Rose Cipollone's case was coming to trial in New Jersey. Merrell Williams was one of a number of paralegals hired by a law firm to sort documents for Brown & Williamson Tobacco Company. In anticipation of lawsuits, the papers were to be sorted according to subject—disease, addiction, failure to warn consumers, safety assurances, work on "safer" cigarettes, marketing to youth. Although most of the papers were boring, Williams saw that some contained information that could be explosive if it became public. From 1988 to 1992, Williams secretly copied thousands of documents from the B&W files.

Those papers remained hidden until 1994, a critical year in which a number of anti-tobacco forces were coming together.

The White House was occupied by Bill Clinton, the nation's first avowedly antismoking president. In February, the federal Food and Drug Administration (FDA) signaled its readiness to take on tobacco for the first time, announcing that it had found evidence that the companies manipulated nicotine levels to satisfy smokers' addiction. In March several new attacks on Big Tobacco were launched. A Florida appeals court cleared the way for the first class-action suit on behalf of nonsmokers who said they had been made sick by environmental, or "secondhand," smoke. In Congress the House Energy and Commerce subcommittee on health and environment opened hearings on regulation of tobacco products.

And in New Orleans that month, dozens of the most successful product liability lawyers in the country filed a megasuit known as *Castano* v. *American Tobacco Company*. Merrell Williams turned his cache of stolen B&W documents over to one of these lawyers.

The third wave of tobacco suits had begun. This one, though, was different from the first two, and it posed a far greater threat to Big Tobacco than anything had in the century since Buck Duke invented the American cigarette industry.

The Castano suit was a national class action, the largest ever mounted against the tobacco industry. A class action is a case in which many people who have suffered similar injuries sue together, thereby spreading the expense and giving the members of the "class" a fairer chance of success. In this case, the lawyers initiated the suit on behalf of a "class" that could include tens of millions of smokers in the United States. The suit focused on addiction, rather than disease—also a new tack. More than sixty lawyers pledged to put $100,000 a year each into a joint fund to finance the Castano suit. For once, the tobacco companies faced adversaries who had the resources and the determination to keep fighting.

The chief executives of the six major cigarette companies and the nation's largest maker of chewing tobacco brought more trouble upon themselves when they appeared before the House health and environment subcommittee that spring. Questioned about whether they believed nicotine was addictive, each stated clearly that he did not believe it. Within weeks, copies of the stolen B&W documents reached

MORE VOICES . . . FROM THE LEGAL RECORD

Congressman Ron Wyden of Oregon:
Let me ask you first, and I'd like to just go down the row, whether each of you believes that nicotine is not addictive?

William I. Campbell, chief executive officer of Philip Morris:
I believe nicotine is not addictive, yes.

James W. Johnston, CEO, R. J. Reynolds:
Congressman, cigarettes and nicotine clearly do not meet the classic definitions of addiction. There is no intoxication.

Joseph Taddeo, CEO, U.S. Tobacco:
I don't believe that nicotine or our products are addicting.

Edward Horrigan, Jr., CEO, Liggett Group:
I believe nicotine is not addictive.

Thomas E. Sandefur, CEO, Brown & Williamson:
I believe nicotine is not addictive.

Donald S. Johnston, CEO, American Tobacco:
And I, too, believe that nicotine is not addictive.

Hearing before the House Energy and Commerce subcommittee on health and the environment, April 14, 1994.[3]

the subcommittee chairman, Congressman Henry Waxman; the papers seemed to show the executives were not being entirely truthful. Soon after, the U.S. Justice Department launched an investigation into whether the seven had committed criminal perjury.

On the heels of the Castano megasuit's filing, a whole new kind of legal attack began in May 1994, when the attorney general of Mississippi sued to get Big Tobacco to reimburse the state for what it had spent on the medical bills of smokers. The tobacco industry had always defended itself by saying that smokers had chosen to take the risk of smoking and were responsible for their own choice. But this was different: The state had not had a choice. It was required by law to pay through the Medicaid program for the medical care of Mississippians who could not pay for it themselves. Within a year, four other states would follow Mississippi's example; eventually, forty states and Puerto Rico would do the same. They charged that the companies had conspired to keep research secret, manipulated nicotine in their products, and intentionally sold cigarettes to children.

These assaults on Big Tobacco by the states, the federal government, and the Castano attorneys grew, overlapped, and fed into each other. More and more documents emerged from industry files to show how the companies had planned together to deny the danger of cigarettes, while their own researchers conducted sophisticated studies into disease, nicotine addiction, and marketing to youths. FDA Commissioner David Kessler got some unexpected help from former employees of Big Tobacco who wanted to blow the whistle on industry manipulation of nicotine. One tipster, still known only as Deep Cough, had been a manager at R. J. Reynolds; another had been B&W's research chief and had been fired after agitating for more research to make cigarettes safer. Before the watershed year 1994 was over, Kessler had learned about a special tobacco, code named Y-1, that B&W had had genetically engineered to contain more than twice the usual amount of nicotine in American tobacco. The seeds had been developed in the United States; B&W had sent them to Brazil, then imported several million pounds of leaf back to the States.

The former B&W scientist, Jeffrey Wigand, explained to the FDA commissioner in detail how cigarette makers controlled the nicotine levels in their products by blending different kinds of leaf. Another important technique was the addition of ammonia, which could increase the amount of nicotine the smoker absorbed. Meanwhile, the stolen B&W documents started turning up everywhere. They were used in a court case for the first time in 1995. Reporters for major newspapers wrote stories from them. By the summer of 1995, the documents were posted on the Internet.

In August of that year, President Clinton announced that the FDA had his approval to regulate cigarettes as a drug delivery device. Clinton presented the move as a public-health initiative to prevent children from starting tobacco use. The proposed FDA rules included a ban on cigarette sales to people under eighteen; a ban on vending machine and mail-order sales of cigarettes; prohibition of cigarette billboards within 1,000 feet (305 meters) of schools; sharp limits on what could be shown in ads in publications with a lot of underage readers; an end to brand-name sponsorship of events or giveaways of merchandise with cigarette logos to children. Within hours of Clinton's announcement, five major cigarette companies sued in North Carolina—where they assumed they would find a judge friendly to tobacco—to stop the FDA rules from taking effect.

Individual lawsuits continued as well, but here, too, things had changed. In 1995 a jury ordered Lorillard to pay $1.3 million in compensatory damages and $700,000 in punitive damages to a man who had gotten lung cancer from smoking Kents when the brand's filters contained asbestos. The next year, a year in which tobacco companies spent more than $657 million on advertising (up from the $512 million they had spent in 1995), another jury awarded damages in a lung cancer case. In this $750,000 verdict against B&W, jurors found that cigarettes are defective products and the manufacturers were negligent. Tobacco companies appealed both verdicts.

Liggett Group, smallest of the cigarette makers, tried to reach an out-of-court settlement with the Castano megasuit attorneys and five of the state attorneys general in 1996. The company's parent firm had other businesses, and Bennett LeBow, the firm's chief executive, hoped the settlement would keep tobacco lawsuits from destroying the entire company. Liggett agreed to put money into stop-smoking programs, limit its advertising and promotions, and provide inside information to those who were suing Big Tobacco. A federal judge dismissed the Castano megasuit in spring 1996, saying the suit was too unwieldy to be tried as a national class action because it involved too many different laws in different states. The Liggett agreement fell through, but Liggett's move dealt a significant blow to the industry. And the Castano attorneys, undeterred by the dismissal of their national case, immediately began filing state class actions.

The pressure on Big Tobacco was widespread and without precedent. Faced with the growing certainty that sooner or later they would have to pay big, tobacco executives still didn't surrender. But they did agree to meet with their adversaries and negotiate.

CHAPTER TEN

SHOWDOWN

The years 1997 and 1998 were roller-coaster times for the tobacco industry in America.

More than 500 law firms and thousands of lawyers were involved on one side or another in the actions against Big Tobacco. The legal bills of the Big Six tobacco companies (Philip Morris, B&W, Lorillard, RJR, American Tobacco, and Liggett) reached about $600 million a year to fight more than 300 suits. If Big Tobacco lost those cases—and by 1997 that was a distinct possibility—it could be forced to pay damages into the hundreds of billions of dollars.

In addition to the changes in anti-tobacco forces, there had been important changes within the companies: The seven executives who had testified before Congress in Congressman Henry Waxman's 1994 hearings were gone. Their successors were willing to consider a compromise with tobacco's enemies in order to keep making money.

So in the first half of 1997, tobacco executives and attorneys engaged in intense, sometimes contentious talks with representatives of the Castano group, the states that were suing, and the federal government. Each side had its own goals: President Clinton, who had sent a representative, wanted to cut the rate of teenage smoking. The states wanted compensation for the Medicaid money they had spent treating sick smokers. The Castano lawyers wanted Big Tobacco to pay for addiction treatment and stop-smoking programs, and they also wanted a big payday. The tobacco companies wanted the lawsuits to stop.

Other developments that spring gave Big Tobacco more nudges toward compromise with the state attorneys general. In March, renegade Liggett settled with twenty states, getting protection from future suits in return for agreeing to provide evidence against the other companies. And in April a federal judge in North Carolina, the heart of tobacco country, ruled that the FDA had the legal authority to define nicotine as a drug, regulate cigarettes as drug delivery devices, and put restrictions on sale and labeling, but not to regulate advertising.

On June 20, 1997, the negotiators announced agreement on a massive national settlement. Under its terms, Big Tobacco would pay $368.5 billion over 25 years. About half would be distributed among all 50 states to cover their tobacco-related costs; $77 billion would go toward lawsuit damages or settlements; $73 billion would be earmarked for public-health measures, including stop-smoking programs and anti-tobacco ads; and $25 billion would go into a trust fund to pay for tobacco-related medical research. The settlement also contained agreement on far-reaching changes in the way the industry did business—provisions that would be the deal's undoing within a year. Big Tobacco agreed to end all billboard ads and sharply limit its magazine advertising; to stop name-brand sponsorship of cultural and sports events, and to stop putting cigarette logos on merchandise such as clothing; to forgo movie product placements (the industry claimed it had not done this in years); to accept some FDA regulation; and to pay penalties of up to $2 billion a year if teenage smoking did not decline by specific percentages. Stores would have to be licensed to sell cigarettes and would have to follow certain rules in displaying tobacco products. In exchange, the industry would be freed of the threat of class-action lawsuits and punitive damage awards (payments intended to punish) for past actions by the companies, and it would not have to pay more than $5 billion in any single year to smokers who won lawsuits.

These last provisions were crucial to the companies. Lawsuit juries had become unpredictable, and the tobacco companies wanted to be able to predict their expenses in order to make plans in their businesses. Furthermore, they hoped to discourage smokers from even attempting to sue. If huge punitive damage awards were not possible, the companies reasoned, then fewer people would be willing to try their luck in court.

But some of the settlement provisions—such as those that involved advertising restrictions, FDA regulation, and limits on civil suits—would require changes in federal law. Thus, the state attorneys general pre-

126

sented the deal to the United States Congress so that it could enact the necessary laws.

While Congress prepared to take up the issue, the existing lawsuits kept grinding on. Big Tobacco settled three state Medicaid suits, agreeing to pay Florida $11.3 billion, Mississippi $3.4 billion, and Texas $15.3 billion. In the fall of 1997 the industry settled its first class-action suit over secondhand smoke. The case, in which Liggett's Bennett LeBow had made his dramatic courtroom statements about the danger of cigarettes, involved about sixty thousand former and current flight attendants. Tobacco companies agreed to spend $300 million for a study of tobacco-related disease, but not to pay the plaintiffs anything.

The winter of 1997–1998 brought more developments that seemed to signal the decline of tobacco. A California biotechnology company that had worked on B&W's Y-1 (high-nicotine tobacco) project agreed to plead guilty to violating export laws and to help the Justice Department in its investigation of the industry. And Lorillard announced that it had lost its appeal of the 1995 Kent/asbestos verdict and had paid $1.5 million to the smoker's survivors.

Minnesota became the first state to bring a Medicaid suit before a jury, rather than settling before its scheduled trial date. The suit accused the cigarette companies and the Tobacco Institute of consumer fraud, false advertising, and antitrust violations. In addition to seeking $1.77 billion, the state asked that Big Tobacco be ordered to open its files on smoking and health research, pay for a public education campaign on the dangers of smoking, prevent sales to minors, fund stop-smoking programs in Minnesota, and shut down the Council for Tobacco Research and the Tobacco Institute. In gathering evidence for its case, the state extracted more than 30 million pages of formerly secret documents from industry files.

After a three-month trial, just as the case was about to be turned over to the jury for a verdict, Minnesota agreed to settle with the industry for $6.6 billion—far more money than the suit had originally asked for. The settlement included more concessions by Big Tobacco than a jury could have ordered. Among the terms:

- No more billboards or ads on buses and taxis.
- No more marketing to children.
- No sales or giveaways of logo merchandise in Minnesota.
- No payments for product placements.
- The Council for Tobacco Research would be dissolved.
- The industry would pay to run a document depository in Minnesota for at least ten years, where about 26 million industry documents would be available for the public to see.

The results of the Minnesota suit were hailed as a major victory by anti-tobacco forces. But while that case had been charging toward its successful resolution, the proposed national settlement had begun falling apart.

Once the settlement became public, it drew attacks from many quarters. Critics noted that sick smokers who wanted to sue Big Tobacco would face the difficult and expensive task of suing alone with a relatively low limit on how much they might be able to collect. FDA Commissioner Kessler thought the agreement did not give the FDA enough authority over cigarettes. Anti-tobacco activists objected to giving the industry protection from lawsuits, something no other corporations had. Some members of Congress wanted to raise taxes on cigarettes. Some wanted to end the tobacco price-support system.

This suggestion brought about a strange alliance of tobacco farmers and some public-health groups. The farmers, of course, did not want to lose the guarantee of decent prices for their crop. If the support program were ended, tobacco farming would no longer be restricted to its traditional home in the East and Southeast. Tobacco could be grown anywhere in the country, by anyone, on any number of acres. The result would probably be a huge increase in the supply of leaf, which would lead to a fall in prices. With the support program in place, farmers could make a living growing as little as 80 to a 100 acres (32 to 40 hectares) of tobacco. Without price supports, farms that small would not survive.

The public-health advocates had a different reason for backing the program. They looked at it as a system for the government to control and set limits

A Powell cartoon offers a ray of hope. The war is not yet over, but the tobacco industry has lost a number of battles, and it looks like its lobbying efforts may not be as powerful as the huge antismoking groundswell. As we enter the twenty-first century, the U.S. government may be able to move forward without the weight of the tobacco industry on its back.

on tobacco production. Their goals were to reduce smoking and discourage young people from starting to smoke. Restricting the supply of tobacco and encouraging higher cigarette prices by keeping the price of leaf up served both of those goals.

By the time a bill was drawn up for Congress to consider, the terms had changed drastically from the settlement the industry had agreed to. The main Senate tobacco bill, sponsored by Senator John McCain of Arizona, called for a tax increase on cigarettes that would raise the price of a pack by about $1.10. The industry's payout over 25 years would be at least $516 billion, not the $368.5 billion in the original settlement. The McCain bill would give the FDA control over cigarettes, fine the companies heavily if youth smoking did not decline enough, and restrict advertising. But the McCain bill eliminated the clause that was so important to Big Tobacco: immunity from future class-action suits.

The tobacco companies revolted. In April 1998—with the Minnesota case still in progress and the debate on the bill in the Senate not yet begun—Big Tobacco announced it no longer wanted any part of the settlement. Speaking for his counterparts at the other major firms, RJR Nabisco's chief Steven F. Goldstone was unequivocal, saying: "The extraordinary settlement reached on June twentieth last year, which could have set the nation on a dramatically new and constructive direction, is dead."[1]

Why should Congress need Big Tobacco's permission to pass laws regulating the industry? Some of the key provisions in the national settlement and in the four-hundred-page McCain bill could have violated the firms' constitutional rights. Restrictions on advertising could well run afoul of First Amendment guarantees of free speech. The steep fines linked to the rate of youth smoking could unfairly penalize the industry for events over which it had no control. And the tobacco companies made it clear they could and would challenge those provisions and tie up the legislation in court for years. History had shown just how tireless Big Tobacco could be in a court battle.

The tobacco legislation's demise offers a stark example of how Congress works. Formal debate began in the Senate on May 18, ten days after Minnesota reached its settlement with the industry. The proposed tobacco bill continued to mutate, as senators grafted new provisions onto it. Among them were some that had nothing to do with tobacco: a new tax deduction for married couples with modest incomes, increased funding to combat drug smuggling, restrictions on loans to students with drug-related convictions, a health insurance tax deduction for self-employed people.

As for the price-support system, two programs were proposed to end it by buying out tobacco quotas. The plans created deep divisions among growers. One program would have paid quota holders $8 a pound; for the owner of 100 acres (40 hectares) of quota, or about 200,000 pounds (90,800 kilograms), that would be a windfall of $1.6 million. Many farmers were willing to accept that buyout and retire, switch crops, or keep growing tobacco without price supports. Smaller growers faced more difficulty. And those who rented rather than owned their quota would get only $4 a pound based on the size of their crops in recent years. An unofficial poll of flue-cured tobacco farmers in May 1998 showed that 80 percent wanted to sell out their quota to the government and let their support program die. The farming community had fought solidly together for decades to preserve the quota system. Now that solidarity was broken.

Just how volatile an issue it was for farmers became obvious at the annual meeting of the Flue-Cured Tobacco Cooperative Stabilization Corporation in Raleigh, North Carolina, that May. Everyone at the meeting shared the goal of doing what was best for tobacco farmers. Yet there was sharp disagreement on what that might be. Jim Graham, agriculture commissioner for North Carolina, stood before the assembly and declared: "The McCain bill must be eliminated." But Bruce Flye, president of the Stabilization Corporation, asserted that if a bill was not passed in Congress in 1998, the continuing uncertainty would destroy some farmers.[2]

The tobacco companies, which had run a nationwide advertising blitz to promote the original settlement, poured money into a campaign to defeat the tobacco bill in Congress. In the space of about two months, Big Tobacco spent $40 million on the effort to convince the public that the bill was no good. The ads portrayed the bill as a $500 billion increase in taxes and claimed it was "opposed by millions of hardworking Americans." Members of Congress who opposed the bill took up this theme, calling the bill a tax on poor people. This was a tricky manipulation of facts: Most cigarettes in the United States are purchased by middle- or low-income consumers. Thus, raising taxes on cigarettes would affect these people the most.

The result was a change in the focus of the debate. Instead of centering on youth-smoking curbs (which voters favored), the argument was now about taxes (which voters shunned). Public support for the bill had been strong at first. Now it eroded. So did support among senators. The tobacco bill had become so loaded down with provisions to suit one constituency or another, that senators declared it unacceptable. On June 16, 1998, not quite a year after Big Tobacco and the state attorneys general announced their sweeping agreement, the settlement died on the Senate floor.

Congress had kept intact its perfect record of never enacting any tobacco control legislation that the industry did not want. The battle returned to the courts.

Tobacco executives vowed that they would fight every lawsuit as aggressively as they always had, and it looked like they would get plenty of opportunity to do so. By the time the McCain bill collapsed, more than eight hundred lawsuits were pending against Big Tobacco, four times as many as there had been only three years earlier. New groups of plaintiffs had joined the fray, including insurance companies and Native American tribes. While the Senate had debated the ill-fated tobacco bill, yet another jury had decided in favor of a smoker's survivors. This $950,000 verdict against Brown & Williamson in Florida had included punitive damages, something that had happened only once before in a tobacco case.

Industry negotiators and lawyers for several states quietly restarted talks about a settlement in the Medicaid cases. This time, the terms under consideration were narrower but still included limits on lawsuits against the industry. Meanwhile, courts threw out the suits filed by the states of Idaho and Indiana.

For a hundred years, the American tobacco industry had emerged victorious from countless attacks. Events in the summer of 1998 raised the possibility that that was about to happen again.

The 1996 Florida jury verdict against Brown & Williamson, awarding a lung cancer victim $750,000, was overturned by an appeals court. B&W then asked a court to overturn the $950,000 judgment it still faced in that state (a request that would be granted in early 1999).

In Greensboro, North Carolina, the same judge who had ruled that the FDA could regulate tobacco decided the Environmental Protection Agency's case against secondhand smoke was shaky. The EPA had declared in 1993 that secondhand smoke causes cancer. The judge's 1998 ruling said the agency had used faulty scientific methods to reach that conclusion. And a federal appeals court tossed out the Greensboro judge's 1996 decision and ruled that the FDA could not regulate tobacco after all.

The tobacco companies abandoned their public attempts to appear conciliatory. R. J. Reynolds launched a defiant new ad campaign for Camel cigarettes, portraying antismoking activists as a bunch of no-fun puritans and playing up the image of smoking as a forbidden pleasure. A similar caustic attitude infused an ad blitz for RJR's Winston brand that featured the slogan "No Bull."

Philip Morris ran sweepstakes for "smokers 21 and over" to win a trip to Marlboro Country—actually, a rented ranch in Arizona or Montana. Marlboro ads urged magazine readers to "Party All Night. Play All Day," and Philip Morris threw Marlboro-themed parties at trendy bars across the country. Attractive male and female models would drive up in red trucks bringing boxes of Marlboro hats, T-shirts, and other free goodies to hand out, but no cigarettes. At the bar parties, the wholesome-looking young adults carefully checked IDs and gathered names and addresses of smokers. At a time when the industry wondered whether even magazine and billboard ads might soon be outlawed, Philip Morris and other cigarette companies used the parties to build lists of people to whom they could mail ads directly.

On November 16, 1998, a group of state attorneys general and the tobacco industry announced a new settlement—one that would not require any action by Congress. Under this agreement, the four biggest tobacco companies (Philip Morris, RJR, Brown & Williamson, and Lorillard) would pay the states about $206 billion over 25 years to compensate for what state governments spent caring for sick smokers. The companies also agreed to accept advertising limits that were more modest than those in the ill-fated 1997 pact: no more billboards or transit signs, no more advertising in sports stadiums, no more product placement in movies or videos, and no more distribution of merchandise bearing cigarette brand logos. They agreed not to use cartoon characters such as the already-defunct Joe Camel but kept the right to use human characters including the Marlboro Man. They would stop hiding information on health effects of smoking, release thousands more documents, shut down the Tobacco Institute, put $250 million into a foundation dedicated to reducing youth smoking, and pay $1.5 billion for an antismoking advertising campaign. In return, the states would drop their Medicaid suits.

Like its predecessors, the new settlement was attacked from many sides. Tobacco state lawmakers noted that the deal held no protection for farmers or quota holders. (Two months later, the companies would agree to set up a $5.15 billion trust fund to help growers and allotment holders.) Public-health leaders said the settlement was not severe enough on the industry. President Clinton renewed his call for FDA control. Nonetheless, all forty-six states that had not previously settled signed on to the new agreement. The companies immediately announced they were raising wholesale prices by forty-five cents a pack, the largest cigarette price increase ever, to cover their settlement costs.

And Philip Morris paid $300 million to Liggett, whose chief executive Bennett LeBow had turned traitor to the industry, to make sure the tiny company joined the settlement and would have to face the same costs and restrictions the other companies faced.

The pact liberated Big Tobacco from its biggest single legal threat, but more court battles lay ahead. The new settlement did not give the companies the provision they had fought so hard for: immunity from class-action suits. Once the state suits were ended, Big Tobacco still faced more than one hundred pending class actions as well as hundreds more suits filed by individuals, unions, pension funds, and local governments. In addition, a new threat sprang up: Foreign governments began to sue the industry, following the example set by the states. Guatemala, Nicaragua, Panama, the Marshall Islands, and British Columbia filed suits. Antismoking advocates hoped these actions would be the beginning of another major assault on the industry.

The U.S. government had not given up either. The Justice Department was continuing its years-long investigation into whether industry executives committed fraud, obstruction into justice, or other crimes. In his 1999 State of the Union speech, President Clinton surprised the industry and its foes by announcing that the Justice Department would file its own suit to recover money the federal government had spent treating smokers' illnesses. And the Supreme Court agreed to decide whether the FDA could regulate tobacco products.

Big Tobacco had come to the end of an important battle with at least a measure of victory. But at the dawn of the new millennium, the war over the industry's future seemed likely to rage on. In February 1999, a San Francisco jury awarded a former smoker $51.5 million in her lawsuit against Philip Morris. The next month a jury in Portland, Oregon, ordered Philip Morris to pay $81 million to the survivors of a smoker who died of lung cancer. The company, as always, said it would appeal both verdicts. The next month, though, an Ohio jury ruled against a group of union insurance funds in a suit modeled after the states' Medicaid suits. Also in March, RJR Nabisco announced it would sell its international tobacco operations to a Japanese tobacco company and would split the conglomerate to make R.J. Reynolds Tobacco a separate company from Nabisco. Days later, RJR sued Philip Morris, claiming its gargantuan rival was illegally monopolizing the market. Ironically, RJR said PM was violating the Sherman Antitrust Act—the same law that had brought about the breakup of Buck Duke's trust and made it possible for R.J. Reynolds to become an industry leader early in the century. Meanwhile, Florida's teen-directed Truth antismoking campaign faced a challenge from lawmakers who wanted to cut off its funding, even though it was less than a year into its planned two-year test period.

Would Big Tobacco rise from the ashes, as it had so many times? Or would tobacco's enemies find a way to leave the industry gasping?

Dr. David Kessler, the former FDA commissioner and now dean of the Yale Medical School, summed up the antismoking camp's determination in the wake of the 1998 settlement: "The day of reckoning for the tobacco industry will come. It may not come this year, it may not come next year, but it will come. I am convinced that we as a country will deal with this deadly product."[3]

VOICES . . . AFTER THE SETTLEMENT

"We believe this agreement represents a step forward in addressing long-standing issues of concern to the states, industry and public. With signing the agreement, the states should be given the opportunity to implement the necessary public health provisions to reduce underage tobacco use."

Joint statement by Philip Morris Inc., R. J. Reynolds Tobacco Company, Brown & Williamson Tobacco Corporation, and Lorillard Tobacco Company, November 23, 1998. [4]

"This is going to go down as one of the biggest con jobs in the history of the world. There are so many adjustments and offsets built into this that I think that over a short period of time, the money is going to disappear."

Stanton A. Glantz, anti-tobacco activist and author, November 23, 1998. [5]

140

Chronology

About 6000 B.C.: Native peoples disperse tobacco throughout the continents now called North and South America. The plant is considered sacred and has many spiritual, social, and medicinal uses.

1492:   Arawak natives in what Europeans call the New World offer Columbus dried tobacco leaves as a gift.

1571:   A respected Spanish physician publishes a history of New World plants in which he calls tobacco "this holy herb" and writes that it can cure many ailments.

1575–1630: Tobacco consumption spreads around the world. The plant is recognized as a cash crop.

1604:   King James I of England issues "A Counterblaste to Tobacco."

1612:   English colonist John Rolfe, better known as the husband of Pocahontas, plants Virginia's first commercial tobacco crop. Tobacco quickly becomes vital to the economic survival of the Colonies.

1665:   The plague rages in Europe. Smoking is thought to prevent the disease.

1761:   A London physician warns against snuff use, reporting ten cases of cancer among snuff users. It is the earliest recorded clinical information on the subject.

1776:   Tobacco trade helps finance the revolution by American colonists.

1828:   German researchers isolate the chemical nicotine and learn that it is highly poisonous.

1839:   Charcoal is used to flue-cure tobacco in Caswell County, North Carolina, resulting in a bright golden, lighter-tasting leaf. "Bright" tobacco will become the dominant cigarette tobacco.

1861–1865: Confederate soldiers in the Civil War get tobacco along with their food rations.

1864:   A mutant strain of tobacco, called White Burley, appears in Ohio. It will become the second-biggest cigarette tobacco.

1866:   Washington Duke and his son, James Buchanan "Buck" Duke, set out to sell the tobacco that remains after Union soldiers loot their farm in Durham's Station, North Carolina. They decide they prefer marketing tobacco to growing it.

1880:   James Albert Bonsack gets a patent for a machine that can make about two hundred cigarettes a minute. Within three years, the machine will be successfully installed in Buck Duke's factory.

1881:   Buck Duke introduces his first cigarette brand, Duke of Durham, and offers small gifts and trading cards to promote it.

Heirs of English tobacconist Philip Morris open a manufacturing plant on Marlborough Street in London.

1889:   Duke makes and sells about half of the 2.1 billion cigarettes consumed in the United States.

1890:   Duke absorbs competitors and incorporates the American Tobacco Company, a "trust" that controls 90 percent of the nation's tobacco market.

1902:   Duke creates the first global trust, British-American Tobacco Company.

Philip Morris & Co. is incorporated in New York and produces a ladies' brand named Marlborough. Two decades later, it will be reintroduced as Marlboro, still a ladies' brand.

1907:   President Theodore Roosevelt launches the government's antitrust prosecution of the American Tobacco Company.

1911:   The Supreme Court rules that American Tobacco is an illegal trust and orders Duke to break it up. The biggest firms to emerge are American Tobacco, Liggett & Myers, and P. Lorillard. Smaller spin-offs include R. J. Reynolds Co. and British-American Tobacco.

1914:   R. J. Reynolds introduces Camel cigarettes, pioneering the American blend of flue-cured and Burley tobaccos.

1914–1918: Cigarettes gain a more masculine image as soldiers in World War I use them.

1915:   Liggett & Myers reformulates its Chesterfield brand to compete with Camels.

1916:   American Tobacco introduces Lucky Strike cigarettes.

1921:   Slogan "I'd Walk a Mile for a Camel" debuts.

Iowa becomes the first state to tax cigarettes.

1923:   Cigarettes become the most popular method of using tobacco in the United States.

1926:   Lorillard introduces Old Gold cigarettes, with the slogan "Not a Cough in a Carload."

1927: British-American Tobacco buys Brown & Williamson Tobacco.

1933: Brown & Williamson introduces menthol-flavored Kool cigarettes.

Tobacco farmers living in poverty ask for government help. The resulting Agricultural Adjustment Act helps raise tobacco prices. With some changes, this tobacco price-support system will remain in place for at least sixty years.

1938: *Consumer Reports* magazine conducts its first test of cigarette ad claims regarding nicotine content and finds that Chesterfield and Marlboro are the strongest.

A Johns Hopkins researcher finds that smokers die younger than nonsmokers.

1939: A German researcher connects the current surge in lung cancer cases with the fact that men started smoking cigarettes in large numbers during World War I.

1941: Cigarettes account for half of Americans' tobacco use.

Reader's Digest, the nation's largest-circulation magazine, criticizes tobacco in an article titled "Nicotine Knockout."

1942: RJR erects smoke-ring-blowing Camel billboard in New York's Times Square.

1950: Three major studies show lung cancer's link to smoking.

1952: The American Cancer Society, with the help of 22,000 volunteers, launches a massive study of smoking and lung cancer.

Lorillard introduces Kent cigarettes, claiming they offer health protection because of their "Micronite" filter. The filter will later be discovered to contain cancer-causing asbestos.

Reader's Digest calls public attention to the danger of lung cancer from smoking.

1953: Researcher Ernst Wynder reports that when he distilled cigarette smoke and painted it on the shaved backs of mice, many got cancerous tumors.

1954: Tobacco companies take out full-page ads headlined "A Frank Statement to Cigarette Smokers" in more than four hundred newspapers to announce the creation of the Tobacco Industry Research Committee (later renamed the Council for Tobacco Research).

Early results from the American Cancer Society study begun in 1952 show a strong link between smoking and lung cancer and for the first time show a connection between smoking and heart disease.

RJR introduces Winston cigarettes.

Philip Morris introduces a new, masculine image for Marlboro. The cowboy will become the most popular character in the brand's ads.

The first product liability suit is filed against the industry, by a smoker's widow. The case will drag on for thirteen years before being dropped.

1964: First surgeon general's report on smoking says cigarettes are a health hazard and calls for "remedial action."

1965: Congress passes a law requiring cigarette packs to carry a label that reads: "Caution: Cigarette Smoking May Be Hazardous to Your Health," and calling for annual reports on smoking from the surgeon general.

1968: Broadcasters are required to provide free airtime for antismoking commercials.

1969: Cigarette package warning labels are toughened to read: "Warning: The Surgeon General has determined that cigarette smoking is dangerous to your health and may cause lung cancer and other diseases."

1971: TV advertising of cigarettes is banned, but the required warning label is toned down.

1972: Commercial airlines are ordered to have nonsmoking sections on all flights; sixteen years later, all smoking will be banned on flights within the United States.

1976: Marlboro becomes the best-selling brand in the United States.

1983: Rose Cipollone, a smoker dying of cancer, sues the tobacco industry.

1984: Four new rotating warning labels are required: "Cigarette Smoke Contains Carbon Monoxide"; "Smoking Causes Lung Cancer, Heart Disease, Emphysema, and May Complicate Pregnancy"; "Smoking by Pregnant Women May Result in Fetal Injury, Premature Birth and Low Birth Weight"; and "Quitting Smoking Now Greatly Reduces Serious Risks to Your Health."

1986: Surgeon general's report says environmental, or "secondhand," tobacco smoke can cause cancer.

Japan, pressured by the Office of the U.S. Trade Representative, agrees to allow the import of American cigarettes. Taiwan and South Korea will follow. Thailand's resistance will spark an anti-tobacco movement in Asia.

1987: Lung cancer overtakes breast cancer as a killer of women.

Merrell Williams is hired to help sort Brown & Williamson documents. Over the next several years, he will secretly copy thousands of them.

1988:   RJR introduces the cartoon Old Joe Camel in its advertising. Nine years later, under pressure from antismoking activists and government regulators, RJR will drop the character.

Rose Cipollone's suit comes to trial, three years after her death. For the first time in a tobacco suit, a jury awards damages—$400,000 to Cipollone's widower. The award will be overturned on appeal.

1990:   Philip Morris spends $30 million to $50 million to sponsor a bicentennial tribute to the Bill of Rights.

1991:   The *Journal of the American Medical Association* reports that almost a third of three-year-olds recognize Joe Camel and that 90 percent of six-year-olds understand the character's connection with cigarettes.

The first class-action suit based on "secondhand" smoke is filed in Florida, on behalf of 60,000 airline flight attendants.

1992:   After almost twenty years of decline, the smoking rate among American teenagers begins to climb, especially among African-American youths.

1993:   The Environmental Protection Agency declares secondhand smoke to be a carcinogen for humans.

February 1994: The Food and Drug Administration announces it has evidence that cigarette companies manipulate nicotine levels.

March 1994: Congressman Henry Waxman opens congressional hearings on tobacco.

The Castano national class-action suit is filed in New Orleans.

April 1994: Seven tobacco company chief executives testify before Waxman's committee that they do not believe nicotine is addictive.

Merrell Williams turns his stolen B&W documents over to a lawyer involved in the Castano megasuit.

May 1994: Mississippi's attorney general sues the tobacco industry to recover money the state has spent, through the Medicaid program, on medical care for sick smokers. Within a year, Florida, Massachusetts, West Virginia, Louisiana, and Texas will file similar suits. It is a new kind of attack on the industry.

1995:   University of California–San Francisco posts the stolen B&W documents on the Internet.

President Bill Clinton orders FDA regulation of cigarettes as drug delivery devices.

A jury awards $1.3 million compensatory and $700,000 punitive damages to Milton Horowitz, who got lung cancer from smoking Kents when their filters contained asbestos. Lorillard appeals the verdict.

1996: Liggett settles with five state attorneys general and agrees to help with their cases against other tobacco companies.

A federal appeals court dismisses the Castano megasuit. The lawyers involved immediately begin filing similar suits in individual states.

A jury awards $750,000 to lung cancer victim Grady Carter. Tobacco companies appeal.

March 1997: Liggett settles with twenty states, gets protection from future suits in return for turning states' evidence.

April 1997: A North Carolina judge rules that the FDA has the authority to regulate cigarettes as drug delivery devices, but not to regulate advertising.

June 20, 1997: Tobacco companies and state attorneys general announce a $368.5 billion national settlement. The agreement requires some changes in federal law and is turned over to Congress.

Summer 1997: Tobacco industry settles Medicaid suits with Florida ($11.3 billion) and Mississippi ($3.3 billion).

October 1997: Tobacco industry settles the flight attendants' class-action suit over secondhand smoke, agreeing to spend $300 million for research into tobacco-related disease.

Winter 1998: California bans smoking in bars.

Lorillard announces it has lost its appeal in the Kent/asbestos case and has paid $1.5 million to Milton Horowitz's family.

Tobacco industry settles Texas Medicaid suit for $15.3 billion.

Trial opens in Minnesota Medicaid suit.

April 1998: Senate Commerce Committee sends a $516 billion tobacco control bill to the full Senate for approval.

Tobacco companies, unhappy with changes the Senate committee has made in the 1997 agreement, withdraw their support of the deal.

Florida launches its teen-directed Truth campaign, with money from the state's tobacco suit settlement. Before the campaign is a year old, some lawmakers will try to yank its funding.

May 1998: Minnesota suit is settled for $6.6 billion.

The Senate begins debate on the McCain tobacco bill.

June 1998: A jury awards $500,000 compensatory and $450,000 punitive damages to the family of lung cancer victim Roland Maddox. Brown & Williamson appeals the verdict.

The McCain tobacco bill, loaded down with provisions unrelated to tobacco, dies in the Senate.

The $750,000 award in the 1996 Grady Carter case is overturned on appeal.

July 1998: A North Carolina judge rules that the EPA's case against secondhand smoke is shaky.

August 1998: A federal appeals court rules that the FDA cannot regulate tobacco after all.

Nebraska becomes the forty-first state to file a Medicaid suit.

November 1998: State attorneys general and tobacco companies announce a new, scaled-back settlement of state Medicaid suits. All 46 states that have not previously settled sign on to the $206 billion pact within a week.

The major cigarette companies raise wholesale prices by a record forty-five cents a pack.

December 1998: The federal government cuts the amount of flue-cured tobacco that can be grown by 18 percent.

January 1999: Tobacco companies agree in principle to start a $5.15 billion trust fund to help growers and quota holders.

President Clinton announces the Justice Department will sue tobacco companies to recover federal money spent treating sick smokers.

Appeals court overturns $950,000 award in the Roland Maddox case, ruling that the lawsuit was tried in the wrong county.

February 1999: A San Francisco jury awards a former smoker $51.5 million in a lawsuit against Philip Morris. PM says it will appeal.

March 1999: RJR Nabisco undoes its 1985 creation, selling its international tobacco operations and splitting R.J. Reynolds Tobacco off as a separate company from Nabisco.

RJR sues Philip Morris, claiming it is trying to shut competitors out of the marketplace.

An Ohio jury rules that a group of union insurance funds cannot collect compensation from tobacco companies for what the funds spent on health care for sick smokers.

Some Florida lawmakers try to end the teen-directed Truth campaign by ending its funding.

A Portland, Oregon, jury orders Philip Morris to pay $81 million to the survivors of a smoker who died of lung cancer. PM says it will appeal.

April 1999: The U.S. Supreme Court agrees to decide whether the FDA can regulate tobacco.

147

Bibliography

Akehurst, B. C. *Tobacco*. New York: Humanities Press, 1968.

American Cancer Society. "Cancer Facts and Figures 1996." Atlanta: American Cancer Society, 1996. Cited from www.cancer.org

American Cancer Society. "Cancer Facts and Figures 1998." Atlanta: American Cancer Society, 1998. Cited from www.cancer.org

American Cancer Society. "Tobacco Information." Fact sheet. Atlanta: Undated, ca. 1996. Cited from www.cancer.org

American Tobacco: How It Is Grown, Cured, Marketed and Processed. N.p.: Tobacco Associates, Inc., and Burley and Dark Leaf Tobacco Export Association, Inc., n.d.

Associated Press, March 10, 1998–April 12, 1999.

Banzhaf, John III. Founder, Action on Smoking and Health. Interview by author. Tape recording. Washington, DC, October 27, 1998.

Barefoot, Pamela. *Mules & Memories*. Winston-Salem, NC: John F. Blair, 1978.

Bloomberg News. February 10–March 13, 1998.

Brooks, Jerome E. *Green Leaf and Gold: Tobacco in North Carolina*. Raleigh, NC: Division of Archives and History, North Carolina Department of Cultural Resources, 1975.

Campaign for Tobacco-Free Kids. "Tobacco Marketing to Kids." Washington, DC: National Center for Tobacco-Free Kids, 1997. Cited from www.tobaccofreekids.org/

Centers for Disease Control and Prevention. "Changes in the Cigarette Brand Preferences of Adolescent Smokers–United States, 1989–1993." *Morbidity and Mortality Weekly Report*, Vol. 43, No. 32, August 19, 1994.

Centers for Disease Control and Prevention. "Selected Cigarette Smoking Initiation and Quitting Behaviors Among High School Students–United States, 1997." *Morbidity and Mortality Weekly Report,* Vol. 47, No. 19, May 22, 1998.

Centers for Disease Control and Prevention. "Incidence of Initiation of Cigarette Smoking–United States, 1965–1996." *Morbidity and Mortality Weekly Report,* Vol. 47, No. 39, October 9, 1998.

Centers for Disease Control and Prevention. Office on Smoking and Health. "Cigarette Smoking-Related Mortality." Tobacco Information and Prevention Source. Atlanta: July 1996. Cited from www.cdc.gov

Centers for Disease Control and Prevention. Office on Smoking and Health. "Tobacco Use Among High School Students–United States, 1997." 1997 Youth Risk Behavior Survey. Atlanta: April 2, 1998. Cited from www.cdc.gov

Clark, Lesley. "State Ads Against Teen Smoking Imperiled." *Miami Herald,* March 13, 1999. Online edition.

Coleman, J. M. Brown & Williamson Tobacco Corp. internal correspondence. Memo to N. V. Domantay. December 5, 1983. Document 2400.13, cited from Tobacco Control Archives, http://galen.library.ucsf.edu/tobacco/

Common Cause. "Tobacco Political Giving Tops $4 Million in 1997, Total Giving Since 1987 Reaches Nearly $30 Million, Common Cause Study Finds." Washington, DC, June 1998. Cited from www.commoncause.org

Congressional Budget Office. "The Proposed Tobacco Settlement: Issues From a Federal Perspective." Report prepared at the request of the Senate assistant majority leader. Washington, DC, April 1998. Cited from www.cbo.gov

Dart, Bob. "Even in Virginia's Capital, Tobacco Heritage Is Under Fire." Cox News Service. May 31, 1998.

Flannagan, Roy. *Golden Harvest: The Way of Life in the Tobacco Industry.* Evanston, IL.: Row, Peterson and Co., 1941.

Flint, Anthony. "Tobacco's World." Parts 1–3. *The Boston Globe,* June 9–11, 1996.

Flue-Cured Tobacco Cooperative Stabilization Corporation. *Annual Report 1998.* Raleigh, NC: Flue-Cured Tobacco Cooperative Stabilization Corporation, 1998.

Frankel, Glenn, James Rupert, and Steven Mufson. "Big Tobacco's Global Reach." Parts 1–4. *The Washington Post,* November 17–20, 1996.

149

Goldberg, Jeffrey. "Big Tobacco's Endgame." *The New York Times Magazine*, June 21, 1998.

Goodman, Jordan. *Tobacco in History: The Cultures of Dependence*. London and New York: Routledge, 1993, 1994.

Hampton, Wade. Interview by author. Tape recording. Albemarle, NC, October 28, 1998.

Hanners, David. "Tobacco Historically Given Little Media Coverage." *St. Paul Pioneer Press*, January 1, 1998.

Hawks, S. N., Jr., and W. K. Collins. *Principles of Flue-Cured Tobacco Production*. Raleigh, NC: Published by S. N. Hawks, Jr., and W. K. Collins, North Carolina State University, 1983.

Heimann, Robert K. *Tobacco and Americans*. New York, Toronto, London: McGraw-Hill Book Co., 1960.

Hilts, Philip J. *Smokescreen: The Truth Behind the Tobacco Industry Cover-Up*. Reading, MA: Addison-Wesley Publishing Co., 1996.

Hohler, Bob. "How the Tobacco Deal Went Up in Smoke." *The Boston Globe*, June 19, 1998.

James I. "A Counterblaste to Tobacco." The English Experience, No. 181. Amsterdam and New York: Da Capo Press, 1969. Originally published London: 1604.

King, Charles III, et al. "Adolescent Exposure to Cigarette Advertising in Magazines: An Evaluation of Brand-Specific Advertising in Relation to Youth Readership." *Journal of the American Medical Association 279* (February 18, 1998): 516–520.

Kluger, Richard. *Ashes to Ashes: America's Hundred-Year Cigarette War, the Public Health, and the Unabashed Triumph of Philip Morris*. New York: Vintage Books/Random House, 1996, 1997.

Krogh, David. *Smoking: The Artificial Passion*. New York: W. H. Freeman and Co., 1991.

LeBow, Bennett. Statement of March 20, 1997. In DIALOG File 610: Business Wire [database online]. 4 screens. Cited May 16, 1998.

Lee, Albert Glen "Toby," and Ray Stanley. Interview by author. New Deal Tobacco Warehouse, Smithfield, NC, October 29, 1997.

Los Angeles Times, April 3–November 16, 1998.

Minneapolis–St. Paul Star Tribune, May 4–July 26, 1998.

Mollenkamp, Carrick, Adam Levy, Joseph Menn, and Jeffrey Rothfeder. *The People vs. Big Tobacco: How the States Took on the Cigarette Giants*. Princeton: Bloomberg Press, 1998.

New York Times, January 15, 1998–January 10, 1999.

Perez, Jared. Interview by author. Tape recording. October 28, 1998.

Philip Morris Companies Inc. *Philip Morris and the Arts: A 30-Year Celebration*. New York: Philip Morris Companies Inc., 1990.

Philip Morris Companies Inc. *1997 Annual Report*. New York: Philip Morris Companies Inc., 1998.

Pierce, John P., et al. "Tobacco Industry Promotion of Cigarettes and Adolescent Smoking." *Journal of the American Medical Association* 279 (February 18, 1998): 511–515.

Pietrusza, David. *Smoking*. Lucent Overview Series. San Diego, CA: Lucent Books, 1997.

Pringle, Peter. *Cornered: Big Tobacco at the Bar of Justice*. New York: Henry Holt and Co., 1998.

Raleigh (N.C.) News & Observer, August 11, 1996–April 27, 1999.

R. J. Reynolds Tobacco Co. *Golden Leaves: R. J. Reynolds Tobacco Company and the Art of Advertising*. New York: R. J. Reynolds Tobacco Co., 1986.

RJR Nabisco Holdings Corp. *RJR Nabisco 1997 Annual Report*. New York: RJR Nabisco Holdings Corp., 1998.

Sherman, Milton M. *All About Tobacco*. N.p., n.d.

Sobel, Robert. *They Satisfy: The Cigarette in American Life*. New York: Anchor/Doubleday, 1978.

Spengler, Pierre. Dovemead Limited. Letter to Phillip (sic) Morris Europe, S.A. October 18, 1979. Accessed from Tobacco Control Archives, http://galen.library.ucsf.edu/tobacco/

Stallone, Sylvester. Letter to Bob Kovoloff, Associated Film Promotion. Los Angeles, CA., April 28, 1983. Document 2406.03, cited from Tobacco Control Archives, http://galen.library.ucsf.edu/tobacco/

Stanley, Ray, and Everett Suitt. Interview by author. Lillington, NC, January 31, 1998.

Thompson, Jackie. Interviews by author. Rolesville, NC, June 1, July 2, September 1, 1998.

Thompson, Jackie. Interview by author. Tape recording. Rolesville, NC, October 20, 1998.

Thompson, Louise Ayscue. Interview by author. Tape recording. Rolesville, NC, July 2, 1998.

Torry, Saundra. "Cigarette Firms Sued by Foreign Governments," *The Washington Post*, January 18, 1999.

U.S. Department of Agriculture. Agricultural Marketing Service–Tobacco Division. "Tobacco Market News." Raleigh, NC, October 9, 1998. Photocopy.

U.S. Department of Agriculture. Economic Research Service. Tobacco Briefing Room: Tobacco Leaf and Products Statistics and Analysis. Washington, D.C., September 21, 1998.

U.S. Department of Agriculture. Economic Research Service. Tobacco Situation and Outlook. Washington, DC, May 1997.

U.S. Department of Agriculture. Economic Research Service. Tobacco Situation and Outlook. Washington, DC, September 1997.

U.S. Department of Agriculture. Economic Research Service. Tobacco Situation and Outlook. Washington, DC, April 1998.

U.S. Department of Agriculture. Economic Research Service. Tobacco Situation and Outlook. Washington, DC, September 1998.

U.S. Department of Agriculture. National Agricultural Statistics Service, Agricultural Statistics Board. Crop Production. Washington, DC, August 12, 1998.

U.S. Department of Health and Human Services. *Tobacco Use Among U.S. Racial/Ethnic Minority Groups: A Report of the Surgeon General.* Washington, DC, April 1998.

U.S. Department of Health and Human Services. Public Health Service, National Institutes of Health. "Nicotine Addiction." National Institute on Drug Abuse Research Report Series. Bethesda, MD, July 24, 1998.
Cited from www.nida.nih.gov/

U.S. Department of Health and Human Services. Substance Abuse and Mental Health Services Administration. 1997 National Household Survey on Drug Abuse. Washington, DC, August 21, 1998.

University of Michigan Institute for Social Research. Monitoring the Future Study. "Smoking Among American Teens Declines Some." December 18, 1998. Cited from www.isr.umich.edu/src/mtf.

Wexler, Celia. Lobbyist and policy analyst, Common Cause. Interview by author. Tape recording. October 29, 1998.

White, Larry C. *Merchants of Death: The American Tobacco Industry.* New York: Beech Tree Books/William Morrow, 1988.

Winkler, John K. *Tobacco Tycoon: The Story of James Buchanan Duke.* New York: Random House, 1942.

World Health Organization. Advisory Kit for World No-Tobacco Day, "Growing Up Without Tobacco." Geneva: May 31, 1998. Cited from www.who.ch/

World Health Organization. "Tobacco Use by Children: A Paediatric Disease." Fact Sheet No. 197. Geneva: May 1998. Cited from www.who.ch/

Yamaguchi, Jean. Electronic mail to author, October 8, 1998.

Source Notes

Chapter 1

1. "Tobacco executive testifies cigarettes are deadly habit," *Raleigh* (N.C.) *News & Observer*, July 22, 1997, in a wire story from Knight-Ridder Newspapers.

2. James Rosen, "Tobacco industry in fight of its life," *Raleigh* (N.C.) *News & Observer*, May 17, 1998.

Chapter 2

1. Jordan Goodman, *Tobacco in History: The Cultures of Dependence* (London and New York: Routledge, 1993, 1994), pp. 44–45. Nicolas Monardes's 1571 history of New World plants credited tobacco with curing more than twenty ailments.

2. John K. Winkler, *Tobacco Tycoon: The Story of James Buchanan Duke* (New York: Random House, 1942), p. 215.

Chapter 4

1. The 1950 studies cited were conducted by Morton L. Levin, Ernst L. Wynder, and the team of Richard Doll and A. Bradford Hill. The 1953 mouse-painting study was conducted by Wynder.

2. Quoted in Richard Kluger, *Ashes to Ashes: America's Hundred-Year Cigarette War, the Public Health, and the Unabashed Triumph of Philip Morris* (New York: Vintage Books/Random House, 1996, 1997), p. 169.

3. Ibid., p. 166.

4. Ibid., p. 258.

5. Statistics cited were compiled from the following sources: American Cancer Society, "Tobacco Information," fact sheet, ca. 1996; "Cancer Facts and Figures 1996" and "Cancer Facts and Figures 1998" (cited from www.cancer.org); Congressional Budget Office, "The Proposed Tobacco Settlement: Issues From a Federal Perspective," report prepared at the request of the Senate assistant majority leader, April 1998 (cited from www.cbo.gov); U.S. Department of Health and Human Services, *Tobacco Use Among U.S.*

Racial/Ethnic Minority Groups: A Report of the Surgeon General, April
1998; Centers for Disease Control and Prevention, Office on
Smoking and Health, "Cigarette Smoking-Related Mortality,"
Tobacco Information and Prevention Source, July 1996 (cited from
www.cdc.gov); Centers for Disease Control and Prevention, "Se-
lected Cigarette Smoking Initiation and Quitting Behaviors
Among High School Students–United States, 1997," *Morbidity and
Mortality Weekly Report* (May 22, 1998), Vol. 47, No. 19; Larry C.
White, *Merchants of Death: The American Tobacco Industry* (New York:
Beech Tree Books/William Morrow, 1988); Laurence Pringle,
Smoking: A Risky Business (New York: Morrow Junior Books, 1996);
Raleigh (N.C.) News & Observer, Associated Press.
6. "Former Beatle Speaks on His Battle Against Throat Cancer,"
   Associated Press, June 28, 1998.

Chapter 5

1. During the 1998 growing season, the author visited Jackie
   Thompson's farm several times and accompanied him to a tobacco auction. The narrative is based on those visits and on the
   author's interviews with Thompson and his mother, Louise A.
   Thompson.

Chapter 6

1. Quoted in Goodman, *Tobacco in History,* p. 191.

Chapter 7

1. Quoted widely, e.g., in World Health Organization Advisory Kit
   for World No-Tobacco Day, "Growing Up Without Tobacco," May
   1998 (cited from www.who.ch/); Jeffrey Goldberg, "Big Tobacco's
   Endgame," *The New York Times Magazine,* June 21, 1998; and Campaign for Tobacco-Free Kids, "Tobacco Marketing to Kids" (National Center for Tobacco-Free Kids, 1997, cited from
   www.tobaccofreekids.org/).
2. Quoted in World Health Organization, "Growing Up Without
   Tobacco," and Campaign for Tobacco-Free Kids, "Tobacco Marketing to Kids."
3. Quoted in Kluger, *Ashes to Ashes,* p. 445.
4. Steve Karnowski, "Tobacco trial continues on two fronts: documents and testimony," Associated Press, March 10, 1998.
5. Quoted in Goldberg, "Big Tobacco's Endgame."
6. The testimony, in Minnesota's suit to recover money spent on
   health care for smokers, was by Cheryl Perry, a specialist in adolescent behavior from the University of Minnesota's School of
   Public Health. Quoted in Karnowski, "Tobacco trial continues."

7. Pierre Spengler, Dovemead Limited, letter to Phillip (sic) Morris Europe, S.A., October 18, 1979; Sylvester Stallone, letter to Bob Kovoloff, Associated Film Promotion, Los Angeles, CA, April 28, 1983 (Document 2406.03); J. M. Coleman, Brown & Williamson Tobacco Corp. internal correspondence, memo to N. V. Domantay, December 5, 1983 (Document 2400.13). The three documents were accessed from Tobacco Control Archives, http://galen.library.ucsf.edu/tobacco/

8. Mike Clary, "Teen-Driven Ad Campaign Puts Heat on Big Tobacco," *Los Angeles Times* (online edition), May 8, 1998.

9. Ibid.

10. Patrick Graham, "Liggett papers show cigarettes aimed at ethnic groups, young," *Raleigh (N.C.) News & Observer*, April 2, 1997, in a wire story from Associated Press.

Chapter 8

1. Glenn Frankel and Steven Mufson, "Vast China Market Key to Smoking Disputes," *The Washington Post*, November 20, 1996.

Chapter 9

1. Quoted in Philip J. Hilts, *Smokescreen: The Truth Behind the Tobacco Industry Cover-Up* (Reading, MA: Addison-Wesley Publishing Co., 1996), pp. 48–50.

2. Quoted in Kluger, *Ashes to Ashes*, p. 676, and Peter Pringle, *Cornered: Big Tobacco at the Bar of Justice* (New York: Henry Holt and Co., 1998), p. 41.

3. Quoted in Philip J. Hilts, *Smokescreen: The Truth Behind the Tobacco Industry Cover-Up* (Reading, MA: Addison-Wesley Publishing Co., 1996), p. 123, and Carrick, Mollenkamp et al., *The People vs. Big Tobacco: How the States Took on the Cigarette Giants* (Princeton: Bloomberg Press, 1998), pp. 50–51.

Chapter 10

1. James Rosen, "Tobacco industry says deal with Congress dead," *Raleigh* (N.C.) *News & Observer*, April 9, 1998.

2. The remarks were made at the Flue-Cured Tobacco Cooperative Stabilization Corporation annual meeting on May 29, 1998, in Raleigh, N.C., which the author attended.

3. James Rosen, "Cigarette makers rise from the ashes, once again," *Raleigh* (N.C.) *News & Observer*, December 2, 1998.

4. "Tobacco Industry Statement," PRNewswire, November 23, 1998.

5. Daniel B. Wood, "Word of caution to spendthrifts," *Christian Science Monitor*, November 23, 1998.

Index

Page numbers in *italics* refer to illustrations.

156